Life After Life and Reflections on Life After Life

by Raymond A. Moody, Jr., M.D.

For the past six years, Dr. Raymond A. Moody, Jr. has interviewed hundreds of men and women who have gone through what is known as "clinical death" and been revived. Their accounts of what it is like to die—and more important, what happens at that moment—are startling, remarkable, revealing and faith-supporting.

LIFE AFTER LIFE
was first published as a straight-forward report on Dr. Moody's studies. But so strong was its appeal that the book quickly became one of the most talked-about nationwide best sellers in years.

In its pages you'll find the astounding true experiences of ordinary people who have stood on the threshold of death and come back changed forever. You'll thrill to the remarkable string of common elements that are found in so many of their stories: the experience of being <u>out</u> of <u>the body</u>...traveling through a <u>dark tunnel</u>...then feeling <u>great peace and tranquility</u>...and most amazing of all, encountering a brilliant <u>being of light</u> whose very presence brings feelings of indescribable love and comfort.

REFLECTIONS ON LIFE AFTER LIFE
is the eagerly-awaited companion book in which Dr. Moody presents additional evidence he has uncovered...plus new material develop...ment a...by LIF...

In this...find ev...mony by people who have come back from the edge of death.

Together, these two extraordinary books are having a profound effect on the way millions regard the promise of eternal life...bringing new understanding to those who doubt and affirmation of faith to those who believe.

RAYMOND A. MOODY, JR. is a psychiatric resident at the University of Virginia Hospital. He is also a philosophy teacher, and has a special interest in ethics, logic, the philosophy of language and the philosophy of medicine.

The latter led him into the study of the phenomena of survival of bodily death, and resulted in his writing of LIFE AFTER LIFE, which became a nationwide best seller. Since then he has spoken around the country to nursing and medical groups, and conducted interviews with people who have had "threshold of death" experiences. This research has been incorporated into his new book, REFLECTIONS ON LIFE AFTER LIFE.

An active Methodist layman, Dr. Moody is married and the father of two sons.

Life After Life
and
Reflections on
Life After Life

by Raymond A. Moody, Jr.

Guideposts

CARMEL • NEW YORK 10512

LIFE
AFTER
LIFE

The investigation of a phenomenon—
survival of bodily death

RAYMOND A. MOODY, JR.

With a foreword by
Elisabeth Kübler-Ross, M.D.

PRINTED IN THE UNITED STATES OF AMERICA

To George Ritchie, M.D.
and, through him, to the
One whom he suggested.

Acknowledgments

There have been very many people who have given me assistance and encouragement during my research and writing, and I could not have completed this project without them. It was my good friend John Ouzts who talked me into giving my first public talk on this subject. John Egle of Mockingbird Books first encouraged me to commit my findings to writing, and has provided support and encouragement throughout. Leonard, Mae, Becky, and Scott Brooks provided room, board, and taxi service for me on many occasions when I needed them. Kathy Tabakian accompanied me on several interviews, and I benefited from long discussions of them with her. Russ Moores, Richard Martin, and Ed McCranie, all of the Medical College of Georgia, offered valuable suggestions and referred me to much relevant literature. My wife spent long hours editing the manuscript and typescript. Finally, I should like most of all to thank all those who told me of their encounters with death. I can only hope that this book is worthy of all the confidence that everyone mentioned above has placed in me.

CONTENTS

Foreword

I have had the privilege of reading the pre-publication copy of Dr. Moody's *Life After Life*, and I am delighted that this young scholar has the courage to put his findings together and make this new type of research available to the general public.

Since I have worked with terminally ill patients over the last two decades, I have become more and more preoccupied with looking into the phenomena of death itself. We have learned a lot about the process of dying, but we still have many questions with regard to the moment of death and to the experience our patients have when they are pronounced medically dead.

It is research such as Dr. Moody presents in his book that will enlighten many and will confirm what we have been taught for two thousand years—that there is life after death. Though he does not claim to have studied death itself, it is evident from his findings that the dying patient continues to have a conscious awareness of his environment after being pronounced clinically dead. This very much coincides with my own research, which has used the accounts of patients who have died and made a comeback, totally against our expectations and often to the surprise of some highly sophisticated, well-known and certainly accomplished physicians.

All of these patients have experienced a floating out of their physical bodies, associated with a great sense of peace and wholeness. Most were aware of another person who helped them in their transition to another plane of existence. Most were greeted by loved ones who had died before them, or by a religious figure who was significant in their life and who coincided, naturally, with their own religious beliefs. It is enlightening to read Dr. Moody's book at the time when I am ready to put my own research findings on paper.

Dr. Moody will have to be prepared for a lot of criticism, mainly from two areas. There will be members of the clergy who will be upset by anyone who dares to do research in an area which is supposed to be taboo. Some religious representatives of a denominational church have already expressed their criticism of studies like this. One priest referred to it as "selling cheap grace." Others simply felt that the question of life after death should remain an issue of blind faith and should not be questioned by anyone. The second group of people that Dr. Moody can expect to respond to his book with concern are scientists and physicians who regard this kind of study as "unscientific."

I think we have reached an era of transition in our society. We have to have the courage to open new doors and admit that our present-day scientific tools are inadequate for many of these new investigations. I think that this book will open these new doors for people who can have an open mind, and it will give them hope and courage to evaluate new areas of research. They will know that this account of Dr. Moody's findings is true, because it is written by a genuine and honest investigator. It is also corroborated by my own research and by the findings of other very serious-minded scientists, scholars and members of the clergy who have had the courage to investigate in this new field of research in the hope of helping those who need to know, rather than to believe.

I recommend this book to anyone with an open mind, and I congratulate Dr. Moody for the courage to put his findings into print.

ELISABETH KÜBLER-ROSS, M.D.

Flossmoor, Illinois

Introduction

T his book, written as it is by a human being, naturally
reflects the background, opinions and prejudices of its
author. So, although I have tried to be as objective and
straightforward as I can, certain facts about me might be useful
in evaluating some of the extraordinary claims which are made
in what follows.

First of all, I have never been close to death myself, so I am
not giving a firsthand account of experiences which I have had
myself. At the same time I cannot claim total objectivity on that
basis, since my emotions have become involved in this project.
In hearing so many people relate the fascinating experiences
with which this volume deals, I have come to feel almost as
though I have lived through them myself. I can only hope that
this attitude has not compromised the rationality and balance of
my approach.

Secondly, I write as a person who is not broadly familiar with
the vast literature on paranormal and occult phenomena. I do
not say this to disparage it, and I feel confident that a wider
acquaintance with it might have increased my understanding of
the events I have studied. In fact, I intend now to look more
closely at some of these writings to see to what extent the
investigations of others are borne out by my findings.

Thirdly, my religious upbringing deserves some comment.

My family attended the Presbyterian Church, yet my parents never tried to impose their religious beliefs or concepts upon their children. They generally tried, as I was growing up, to encourage whatever interests I developed on my own and provided the opportunity for me to pursue them. So, I have grown up having a "religion" not as a set of fixed doctrines, but rather as a concern with spiritual and religious doctrines, teachings, and questions. I believe that all the great religions of man have many truths to tell us, and I believe that no one of us has all the answers to the deep and fundamental truths with which religion deals. In organizational terms, I am a member of the Methodist Church.

Fourthly, my academic and professional background is somewhat diverse—some would say fractured. I attended graduate school in philosophy at the University of Virginia and received my Ph.D. in that subject in 1969. My areas of special interest in philosophy are ethics, logic, and the philosophy of language. After teaching philosophy for three years at a university in eastern North Carolina, I decided to go to medical school, and I intend to become a psychiatrist and to teach the philosophy of medicine in a medical school. All these interests and experiences necessarily helped shape the approach I have taken in this study.

My hope for this book is that it will draw attention to a phenomenon which is at once very widespread and very well-hidden, and, at the same time, help create a more receptive public attitude toward it. For it is my firm conviction that this phenomenon has great significance, not only for many academic and practical fields—especially psychology, psychiatry, medicine, philosophy, theology, and the ministry—but also for the way in which we lead our daily lives.

Let me say at the very beginning that, on grounds which I will explain much later, I am not trying to prove that there is life after death. Nor do I think that a "proof" of this is presently possible. Partly for this reason, I have avoided the use of actual names and have disguised certain identifying details in the stories, while leaving their contents unchanged. This has been necessary, both to protect the privacy of the individuals concerned and, in many cases, to be granted permission to publish the experience related to me in the first place.

There will be many who will find the claims made in this book incredible and whose first reaction will be to dismiss them out of hand. I have no room whatsoever to blame anyone who finds himself in this category; I would have had precisely the same reaction only a few years ago. I am not asking that anyone accept and believe the contents of this volume on my authority alone. Indeed, as a logician who disavows that road to belief which proceeds through invalid appeals to authority, I specifically ask that no one do so. All I ask is for anyone who disbelieves what he reads here to poke around a bit for himself. I have issued this challenge repeatedly for some time. Of those who have accepted it, there have been very many who, skeptical at first, have come to share my bafflement over these events.

On the other hand, there no doubt will be many who read this and find in it a great relief, for they will discover that they are not alone in having had such an experience. To them— especially if, like most, they have concealed their story from all but a few trusted persons—I can only say this: It is my hope that this volume may encourage you to speak a little more freely, so that a most intriguing facet of the human soul may be more clearly elucidated.

I.
THE PHENOMENON OF DEATH

What is it like to die?

That is a question which humanity has been asking itself ever since there have been humans. Over the past few years, I have had the opportunity to raise this question before a sizable number of audiences. These groups have ranged from classes in psychology, philosophy, and sociology through church organizations, television audiences, and civic clubs to professional societies of medicine. On the basis of this exposure, I can safely say that this topic excites the most powerful of feelings from people of many emotional types and walks of life.

Yet, despite all this interest it remains true that it is very difficult for most of us to talk about death. There are at least two reasons for this. One of them is primarily psychological and cultural: The subject of death is taboo. We feel, perhaps only subconsciously, that to be in contact with death in any way, even indirectly, somehow confronts us with the prospect of our own deaths, draws our own deaths closer and makes them more real and thinkable. For example, most medical students, myself included, have found that even the remote encounter with death which occurs upon one's first visit to the anatomical laboratories when entering medical school can evoke strong feelings of uneasiness. In my own case, the reason for this response now seems quite obvious. It has occurred to me in retrospect that it wasn't entirely concern for the person whose remains I saw there, although that feeling certainly figured, too. What I was seeing on that table was a symbol of my own mortality. In some way, if only pre-consciously, the thought must have been in my mind, "That will happen to me, too."

Likewise, talking about death can be seen on the psychological level as another way of approaching it indirectly. No doubt many people have the feeling that to talk about death at all is in effect to conjure it up mentally, to bring it closer in such a way that one has to face up to the inevitability of one's own eventual demise. So, to spare ourselves this psychological trauma, we decide just to try to avoid the topic as much as possible.

The second reason it is difficult to discuss death is more complicated, as it is rooted in the very nature of language itself. For the most part, the words of human language allude to things of which we have experience through our own physical senses. Death, though, is something which lies beyond the conscious experience of most of us because most of us have never been through it.

If we are to talk about death at all, then, we must avoid both social taboos and the deep-seated linguistic dilemmas which derive from our own inexperience. What we often end up doing is talking in euphemistic analogies. We compare death or dying with more pleasant things in our experience, things with which we are familiar.

Perhaps the most common analogy of this type is the comparison between death and sleep. Dying, we tell ourselves, is like going to sleep. This figure of speech occurs very commonly in everyday thought and language, as well as in the literature of many cultures and many ages. It was apparently quite common even in the time of the ancient Greeks. In *The Iliad*, for example, Homer calls sleep "death's sister," and Plato, in his dialogue *The Apology*, put the following words into the mouth of his teacher, Socrates, who has just been sentenced to death by an Athenian jury.

> [Now, if death is only a dreamless sleep,] it must be a marvelous gain. I suppose that if anyone were told to pick out the night on which he slept so soundly as not even to dream, and then to compare it with all the other nights and days of his life, and then were told to say, after due consideration, how many better and happier days and nights than this he had spent in the course of his life—well, I think that . . . [anyone] would find these days and nights easy to count in comparison with the rest. If death is like this, then, I call it gain, because the whole of time, if you look at it in this way, can be regarded as no more than one single night.[1]

This same analogy is embedded in our own contemporary language. Consider the phrase "to put to sleep." If you present your dog to a veterinarian with the instruction to put him to sleep, you would normally mean something very different than you would upon taking your wife or husband to an anesthesiologist with the same words. Others prefer a different, but related analogy. Dying, they say, is like forgetting. When one dies, one forgets all one's woes; all one's painful and troubling memories are obliterated.

As old and as widespread as they may be, however, both the "sleeping" and the "forgetting" analogies are ultimately inadequate in so far as comforting us is concerned. Each is a different way of making the same assertion. Even though they tell us so in a somewhat more palatable way, both say, in effect, that death is simply the annihilation of conscious experience, forever. If this is so, then death really doesn't have any of the desirable features of sleeping and forgetting. Sleeping is a positive, desirable experience in life because waking follows it.

A restful night's sleep makes the waking hours following it more pleasant and productive. If waking did not follow it, the benefits of sleep would not be possible. Similarly, annihilation of all conscious experience implies not only the obliteration of all painful memories, but of all pleasant ones, too. So upon analysis, neither analogy is close enough to give us any real comfort or hope in facing death.

There is another view, however, which disavows the notion that death is annihilation of consciousness. According to this other, perhaps more ancient tradition, some aspect of the human being survives even after the physical body ceases to function and is ultimately destroyed. This persistent aspect has been called by many names, among them psyche, soul, mind, spirit, self, being, and consciousness. By whatever name it is called, the notion that one passes into another realm of existence upon physical death is among the most venerable of human beliefs. There is a graveyard in Turkey which was used by Neanderthal men approximately 100,000 years ago. There, fossilized imprints have enabled archaeologists to discover that these ancient men buried their dead in biers of flowers, indicating that they perhaps saw death as an occasion of celebration—as a transition of the dead from this world to the next. Indeed, graves from very early sites all over the earth give evidence of the belief in human survival of bodily death.

In short, we are faced with two contrasting answers to our original question about the nature of death, both of ancient derivation, yet both widely held even today. Some say that death is annihilation of consciousness; others say with equal confidence that death is the passage of the soul or mind into another dimension of reality. In what follows I do not wish in any way to dismiss either answer. I simply wish to give a report on a search which I have personally undertaken.

During the past few years I have encountered a large number of persons who were involved in what I shall call "near-death experiences." I have met these persons in many ways. At first it was by coincidence. In 1965, when I was an undergraduate student studying philosophy at the University of Virginia, I met a man who was a clinical professor of psychiatry in the School of Medicine. I was struck from the beginning with his warmth, kindliness and humor. It came as a great surprise when I later learned a very interesting fact about him, namely, that he had been dead—not just once but on two occasions, about ten minutes apart—and that he had given a most fantastic account of what happened to him while he was "dead." I later heard him relate his story to a small group of interested students. At the time, I was most impressed, but since I had little background from which to judge such experiences, I "filed it away," both in my mind and in the form of a tape recording of his talk.

Some years later, after I had received my Ph.D. in philosophy, I was teaching in a university in eastern North Carolina. In one course I had my students read Plato's *Phaedo*, a work in which immortality is among the subjects discussed. In my lectures I had been emphasizing the other doctrines which Plato presents there and had not focused upon the discussion of life after death. After class one day a student stopped by to see me. He asked whether we might discuss the subject of immortality. He had an interest in the subject because his grandmother had "died" during an operation and had recounted a very amazing experience. I asked him to tell me about it, and much to my surprise, he related almost the same series of events which I had heard the psychiatry professor describe some years before.

At this time my search for cases became a bit more active, and I began to include readings on the subject of human survival of biological death in my philosophy courses. However, I was careful not to mention the two death experiences in my courses. I adopted, in effect, a wait-and-see attitude. If such reports were fairly common, I thought, I would probably hear of more if I just brought up the general topic of survival in philosophical discussions, expressed a sympathetic attitude toward the question, and waited. To my amazement, I found that in almost every class of thirty or so students, at least one student would come to me afterwards and relate a personal near-death experience.

What has amazed me since the beginning of my interest are

the great similarities in the reports, despite the fact that they come from people of highly varied religious, social, and educational backgrounds. By the time I entered medical school in 1972, I had collected a sizable number of these experiences and I began mentioning the informal study I had been doing to some of my medical acquaintances. Eventually, a friend of mine talked me into giving a report to a medical society, and other public talks followed. Again, I found that after every talk someone would come up to tell me of an experience of his own.

As I became more widely known for this interest, doctors began to refer to me persons whom they had resuscitated and who reported unusual experiences. Still others have written to me with reports after newspaper articles about my studies appeared.

At the present time, I know of approximately 150 cases of this phenomenon. The experiences which I have studied fall into three distinct categories:

(1) The experiences of persons who were resuscitated after having been thought, adjudged, or pronounced clinically dead by their doctors.

(2) The experiences of persons who, in the course of accidents or severe injury or illness, came very close to physical death.

(3) The experiences of persons who, as they died, told them to other people who were present. Later, these other people reported the content of the death experience to me.

From the vast amount of material that could be derived from 150 cases, selection obviously has occurred. Some of it has been purposeful. For example, although I have found reports of the third type to complement and to agree very well with experiences of the first two types, I have for the most part dropped them from consideration for two reasons. First, it helps to reduce the number of cases studied to a more manageable level, and second, it enables me to stick as close as possible to firsthand reports. Thus, I have interviewed in great detail some fifty persons upon whose experiences I am able to report. Of these, the cases of the first type (those in which an apparent clinical death actually occurs) are certainly more *dramatic* than those of the second type (in which only a close brush with death occurs). Indeed, whenever, I have given public talks on this phenomenon, the "death" episodes have invariably drawn most of the interest. Accounts in the press have sometimes been written so as to suggest they are the *only* type of case with which I have dealt.

However, in selecting the cases to be presented in this book, I have avoided the temptation to dwell only on those cases in which a "death" event took place. For, as will become obvious, cases of the second type are not different from, but rather form a continuum with, cases of the first type. Also, though the near-death experiences themselves are remarkably similar, both the circumstances surrounding them and the persons describing them vary widely. Accordingly, I have tried to give a sample of experiences which adequately reflects this variation. With these qualifications in mind, let us now turn to a consideration of what may happen, as far as I have been able to discover, during the experience of dying.

---

[1]Plato, *The Last Days of Socrates*, trans. Hugh Tredennick (Baltimore: Penguin Books, 1959), p. 75

II.
THE EXPERIENCE
OF DYING

Despite the wide variation in the circumstances surrounding close calls with death and in the types of persons undergoing them, it remains true that there is a striking similarity among the accounts of the experiences themselves. In fact, the similarities among various reports are so great that one can easily pick out about fifteen separate elements which recur again and again in the mass of narratives that I have collected. On the basis of these points of likeness, let me now construct a brief, theoretically "ideal" or "complete" experience which embodies all of the common elements, in the order in which it is typical for them to occur.

A man is dying and, as he reaches the point of greatest physical distress, he hears himself pronounced dead by his

*doctor. He begins to hear an uncomfortable noise, a loud
ringing or buzzing, and at the same time feels himself moving
very rapidly through a long dark tunnel. After this, he suddenly finds himself outside of his own physical body, but still in
the immediate physical environment, and he sees his own body
from a distance, as though he is a spectator. He watches the
resuscitation attempt from this unusual vantage point and is in
a state of emotional upheaval.*

*After a while, he collects himself and becomes more accus-
tomed to his odd condition. He notices that he still has a "body,"
but one of a very different nature and with very different
powers from the physical body he has left behind. Soon other
things begin to happen. Others come to meet and to help him.
He glimpses the spirits of relatives and friends who have already died, and a loving, warm spirit of a kind he has never
encountered before—a being of light—appears before him. This
being asks him a question, nonverbally, to make him evaluate
his life and helps him along by showing him a panoramic,
instantaneous playback of the major events of his life. At some
point he finds himself approaching some sort of barrier or
border, apparently representing the limit between earthly life
and the next life. Yet, he finds that he must go back to the earth,
that the time for his death has not yet come. At this point he
resists, for by now he is taken up with his experiences in the
afterlife and does not want to return. He is overwhelmed by
intense feelings of joy, love, and peace. Despite his attitude,
though, he somehow reunites with his physical body and lives.*

*Later he tries to tell others, but he has trouble doing so. In
the first place, he can find no human words adequate to describe these unearthly episodes. He also finds that others scoff,
so he stops telling other people. Still, the experience affects his
life profoundly, especially his views about death and its relationship to life.*

It is important to bear in mind that the above narrative is not
meant to be a representation of any one person's experience.
Rather, it is a "model," a composite of the common elements
found in very many stories. I introduce it here only to give a

preliminary, general idea of what a person who is dying may experience. Since it is an abstraction rather than an actual account, in the present chapter I will discuss in detail each common element, giving many examples.

Before doing that, however, a few facts need to be set out in order to put the remainder of my exposition of the experience of dying into the proper framework.

(1) Despite the striking similarities among various accounts, no two of them are precisely identical (though a few come remarkably close to it).

(2) I have found no one person who reports every single component of the composite experience. Very many have reported most of them (that is, eight or more of the fifteen or so) and a few have reported up to twelve.

(3) There is no one element of the composite experience which every single person has reported to me, which crops up in every narrative. Nonetheless, a few of these elements come fairly close to being universal.

(4) There is not one component of my abstract model which has appeared in only one account. Each element has shown up in many separate stories.

(5) The order in which a dying person goes through the various stages briefly delineated above may vary from that given in my "theoretical model." To give one example, various persons have reported seeing the "being of light" before, or at the same time, they left their physical bodies, and not as in the "model," some time afterward. However, the order in which the stages occur in the model is a very typical order, and wide variations are unusual.

(6) How far into the hypothetical complete experience a dying person gets seems to depend on whether or not the

person actually underwent an apparent clinical death, and if so, on how long he was in this state. In general, persons who were "dead" seem to report more florid, complete experiences than those who only came close to death, and those who were "dead" for a longer period go deeper than those who were "dead" for a shorter time.

(7) I have talked to a few people who were pronounced dead, resuscitated, and came back reporting none of these common elements. Indeed, they say that they don't remember anything at all about their "deaths." Interestingly enough, I have talked with several persons who were actually adjudged clinically dead on separate occasions years apart, and reported experiencing nothing on one of the occasions, but having had quite involved experiences on the other.

(8) It must be emphasized that I am writing primarily about reports, accounts, or narratives, which other persons have given to me verbally during interviews. Thus, when I remark that a given element of the abstract, "complete" experience does not occur in a given account, I do not mean necessarily to imply that it did not happen to the person involved. I only mean that this person did not tell me that it did occur, or that it does not definitely come out in his account that he experienced it. Within this framework, then, let us look at some of the common stages and events of the experiences of dying.

Ineffability

The general understanding we have of language depends upon the existence of a broad community of common experience in which almost all of us participate. This fact creates an important difficulty which complicates all of the discussion which is to follow. The events which those who have come near death have lived through lie outside our community of experience, so one might well expect that they would have some linguistic difficulties in expressing what happened to them. In fact, this is precisely the case. The persons involved uniformly characterize their experiences as ineffable, that is, "inexpressible."

Many people have made remarks to the effect that, "There are just no words to express what I am trying to say," or "They just don't make adjectives and superlatives to describe this." One woman put this to me very succinctly when she said:

Now, there is a real problem for me as I'm trying to tell you this, because all the words I know are three-dimensional. As I was going through this, I kept thinking, "Well, when I was taking geometry, they always told me there were only three dimensions, and I always just accepted that. But they were wrong. There are more." And, of course, our world—the one we're living in now—*is* three-dimensional, but the next one definitely isn't. And that's why it's so hard to tell you this. I have to describe it to you in words that are three-dimensional. That's as close as I can get to it, but it's not really adequate. I can't really give you a complete picture.

Hearing The News

Numerous people have told of hearing their doctors or other spectators in effect pronounce them dead. One woman related to me that,

I was in the hospital, but they didn't know what was wrong with me. So Dr. James, my doctor, sent me downstairs to the radiologist for a liver scan so they could find out. First, they tested this drug they were going to use on my arm, since I had a lot of drug allergies. But there was no reaction, so they went ahead. When they used it this time, I arrested on them. I heard the radiologist who was working on me go over to the telephone, and I heard very clearly as he dialed it. I heard him say, "Dr. James, I've killed your patient, Mrs. Martin." And I knew I wasn't dead. I tried to move or to let them know, but I couldn't. When they were trying to resuscitate me, I could hear them telling how many c.c.'s of something to give me, but I didn't feel the needles going in. I felt nothing at all when they touched me.

In another case, a woman who had previously had several episodes of heart trouble was seized with a heart attack, during which she nearly lost her life. She says,

Suddenly, I was gripped by squeezing chest pains, just as though an iron band had been clamped quickly around the middle part of my chest and tightened. My husband and a friend of ours heard me fall and came running in to help me. I found myself in a deep blackness, and through it I heard my husband, as if he were at a great distance, saying, "This is it, this time!" And my thoughts were, "Yes, it is."

A young man who was thought dead following an automobile accident says, "I heard a woman who was there say, 'Is he dead?' and someone else said, 'Yeah, he's dead'."

Reports of this type accord quite well with what the doctors and others present remember. For example, one doctor told me,

A woman patient of mine had a cardiac arrest just before another surgeon and I were to operate on her. I was right there, and I saw her pupils dilate. We tried for some time to resuscitate her, but weren't having any success, so I thought she was gone. I told the other doctor who was working with me, "Let's try one more time and then we'll give up." This time, we got her heart beating, and she came around. Later I asked her what she remembered of her "death." She said she didn't remember much about it, except that she did hear me say, "Let's try one more time and then we'll give up."

Feelings of Peace and Quiet

Many people describe extremely pleasant feelings and sensations during the early stages of their experiences. After a severe head injury, one man's vital signs were undetectable. As he says,

At the point of injury there was a momentary flash of pain, but then all the pain vanished. I had the feeling of floating in a dark space. The day was bitterly cold, yet while I was in that blackness all I felt was warmth and the most extreme comfort I have ever experienced. . . . I remember thinking, "I must be dead."

A woman who was resuscitated after a heart attack remarks,

I began to experience the most wonderful feelings. I couldn't feel a thing in the world except peace, comfort, ease—just quietness. I felt that all my troubles were gone, and I thought to myself, "Well how quiet and peaceful, and I don't hurt at all."

Another man recalls,

I just had a nice, great feeling of solitude and peace . . . It was beautiful, and I was at such peace in my mind.

A man who "died" after wounds suffered in Viet Nam says that as he was hit he felt

A great attitude of relief. There was no pain, and I've never felt so relaxed. I was at ease and it was all good.

The Noise

In many cases, various unusual auditory sensations are reported to occur at or near death. Sometimes these are extremely unpleasant. A man who "died" for twenty minutes during an abdominal operation describes "a really bad buzzing noise coming from inside my head. It made me very uncomfortable. . . . I'll never forget that noise." Another woman tells how as she lost consciousness she heard "a loud ringing. It could be described as a buzzing. And I was in a sort of whirling state." I have also heard this annoying sensation described as a loud click, a roaring, a banging, and as a "whistling sound, like the wind."

In other cases the auditory effects seem to take a more pleasant musical form. For example, a man who was revived after having been pronounced dead on arrival at the hospital recounts that during his death experience,

> I would hear what seemed to be bells tingling, a long way off, as if drifting through the wind. They sounded like Japanese wind bells. . . . That was the only sound I could hear at times.

A young woman who nearly died from internal bleeding associated with a blood clotting disorder says that at the moment she collapsed, "I began to hear music of some sort, a majestic, really beautiful sort of music."

The Dark Tunnel

Often concurrently with the occurrence of the noise, people have the sensation of being pulled very rapidly through a dark space of some kind. Many different words are used to describe this space. I have heard this space described as a cave, a well, a trough, an enclosure, a tunnel, a funnel, a vacuum, a void, a sewer, a valley, and a cylinder. Although people use different terminology here, it is clear that they are all trying to express some one idea. Let us look at two accounts in which the "tunnel" figures prominently.

This happened to me when I was a little boy—nine years old. That was twenty-seven years ago, but it was so striking that I have never forgotten it. One afternoon I became very sick, and they rushed me to the nearest hospital. When I arrived they decided they were going to have to put me to sleep, but why I don't know, because I was too young. Back in those days they used ether. They gave it to me by putting a cloth over my nose, and when they did, I was told afterwards, my heart stopped beating. I didn't know at that time that that was exactly what happened to me, but anyway when this happened I had an experience. Well, the first thing that happened—now I am going to describe it just the way I felt—was that I had this ringing noise brrrrrrnnnnng-brrrrrrnnnnng-brrrrrrnnnnng, very rhythmic. Then I was moving through this—you're going to think this is weird—through this long dark place. It seemed like a sewer or something. I just can't describe it to you. I was moving, beating all the time with this noise, this ringing noise.

Another informant states:

I had a very bad allergic reaction to a local anesthetic, and I just quit breathing—I had a respiratory arrest. The first thing that happened—it was real quick—was that I went through this dark, black vacuum at super speed. You could compare it to a tunnel, I guess. I felt like I was riding on a roller coaster train at an amusement park, going through this tunnel at a tremendous speed.

During a severe illness, a man came so near death that his pupils dilated and his body was growing cold. He says,

I was in an utterly black, dark void. It is very difficult to explain, but I felt as if I were moving in a vacuum, just through blackness. Yet, I was quite conscious. It was like being in a cylinder which had no air in it. It was a feeling of limbo, of being half-way here, and half-way somewhere else.

A man who "died" several times after severe burns and fall injuries says,

I stayed in shock for about a week, and during that time all of a sudden I just escaped into this dark void. It seemed that I stayed there for a long time just floating and tumbling through space. . . . I was so taken up with this void that I just didn't think of anything else.

Before the time of his experience, which took place when he was a child, one man had had a fear of the dark. Yet, when his heart stopped beating from internal injuries incurred in a bicycle accident,

I had the feeling that I was moving through a deep, very dark valley. The darkness was so deep and impenetrable that I could see absolutely nothing but this was the most wonderful, worry-free experience you can imagine.

In another case, a woman had had peritonitis, and relates,

My doctor had already called my brother and sister in to see me for the last time. The nurse gave me a shot to help me die more easily. The things around me in the hospital began to get further and further away. As they receded, I entered head first into a narrow and very, very dark passageway. I seemed to just fit inside of it. I began to slide down, down, down.

One woman, who was near death following a traffic accident, drew a parallel from a television show.

There was a feeling of utter peace and quiet, no fear at

all, and I found myself in a tunnel—a tunnel of concentric circles. Shortly after that, I saw a T.V. program called *The Time Tunnel*, where people go back in time through this spiralling tunnel. Well, that's the closest thing to it that I can think of.

A man who came very near death drew a somewhat different parallel, one from his religious background. He says,

Suddenly, I was in a very dark, very deep valley. It was as though there was a pathway, almost a road, through the valley, and I was going down the path. . . . Later, after I was well, the thought came to me, "Well, now I know what the Bible means by 'the valley of the shadow of death,' because I've been there."

Out Of The Body

It is a truism that most of us, most of the time, identify ourselves with our physical bodies. We grant, of course, that we have "minds," too. But to most people our "minds" seem much more ephemeral than our bodies. The "mind," after all, might be no more than the effect of the electrical and chemical activity which takes place in the brain, which is a part of the physical body. For many people it is an impossible task even to conceive of what it would be like to exist in any other way than in the physical body to which they are accustomed.

Prior to their experiences, the persons I have interviewed were not, as a group, any different from the average person with respect to this attitude. That is why, after his rapid passage through the dark tunnel, a dying person often has such an overwhelming surprise. For, at this point he may find himself looking upon his own physical body from a point outside of it, as though he were "a spectator" or "a third person in the room" or watching figures and events "onstage in a play" or "in a movie." Let us look now at portions of some accounts in which these uncanny out-of-the-body episodes are described.

I was seventeen years old and my brother and I were working at an amusement park. One afternoon, we decided to go swimming, and there were quite a few of the other young people who went in with us. Someone said, "Let's swim across the lake." I had done that on numerous occasions, but that day for some reason, I went down, almost in the middle of the lake . . . I kept bobbling up and down, and all of a sudden, it felt as though I were away from my body, away from everybody, in space by myself. Although I was stable, staying at the same level, I saw my body in the water about three or four feet away, bobbling up and down. I viewed my body from the back and slightly to the right side. I still felt as though I had an entire body form, even while I was outside my body. I had an airy feeling that's almost indescribable. I felt like a feather.

A woman recalls,

About a year ago, I was admitted to the hospital with heart trouble, and the next morning, lying in the hospital bed, I began to have a very severe pain in my chest. I pushed the button beside the bed to call for the nurses, and they came in and started working on me. I was quite uncomfortable lying on my back so I turned over, and as I did I quit breathing and my heart stopped beating. Just then, I heard the nurses shout, "Code pink! Code pink!" As they were saying this, I could feel myself moving out of my body and sliding down between the mattress and the rail on the side of the bed—actually it seemed as if I went *through* the rail—on down to the floor. Then, I started rising upward, slowly. On my way up, I saw more nurses come running into the room—there must have been a dozen of them. My doctor happened to be making his rounds in the hospital so they called him and I saw him come in, too. I thought, "I wonder what he's doing here." I drifted on up past the light fixture—I saw it from the side and very distinctly—and then I stopped, floating right below the ceiling, looking down. I felt almost as though I were a piece of paper that someone had blown up to the ceiling.

I watched them reviving me from up there! My body was lying down there stretched out on the bed, in plain view, and they were all standing around it. I heard one nurse say, "Oh, my God! She's gone!", while another one leaned down to give me mouth-to-mouth resuscitation. I was looking at the *back* of her head while she did this. I'll never forget the way her hair looked; it was cut kind of short. Just then, I saw them roll this machine in there, and they put the shocks on my chest. When they did, I saw my whole body just jump right up off the bed, and I heard every bone in my body crack and pop. It was the most awful thing!

As I saw them below beating on my chest and rubbing my arms and legs, I thought, "Why are they going to so much trouble? I'm just fine now."

A young informant states,

It was about two years ago, and I had just turned nineteen. I was driving a friend of mine home in my car, and as I got to this particular intersection downtown, I stopped and looked both ways, but I didn't see a thing coming. I pulled on out into the intersection and as I did I heard my friend yell at the top of his voice. When I looked I saw a blinding light, the headlights of a car that was speeding toward us. I heard this awful sound—the side of the car being crushed in—and there was just an instant during which I seemed to be going through a darkness, an enclosed space. It was very quick. Then, I was sort of floating about five feet above the street, about five yards away from the car, I'd say, and I heard the echo of the crash dying away. I saw people come running up and crowding around the car, and I saw my friend get out of the car, obviously in shock. I could see my own body in the wreckage among all those people, and could see them trying to get it out. My legs were all twisted and there was blood all over the place.

As one might well imagine, some unparalleled thoughts and feelings run through the minds of persons who find themselves in this predicament. Many people find the notion of being out of their bodies so unthinkable that, even as they are experiencing it, they feel conceptually quite confused about the whole thing and do not link it with death for a considerable time. They wonder what is happening to them; why can they suddenly see themselves from a distance, as though a spectator?

Emotional responses to this strange state vary widely. Most people report, at first, a desperate desire to get back into their bodies but they do not have the faintest idea about how to proceed. Others recall that they were very afraid, almost panicky. Some, however, report more positive reactions to their plight, as in this account:

> I became very seriously ill, and the doctor put me in the hospital. This one morning a solid gray mist gathered around me, and I left my body. I had a floating sensation as I felt myself get out of my body, and I looked back and I could see myself on the bed below and there was no fear. It was quiet—very peaceful and serene. I was not in the least bit upset or frightened. It was just a tranquil feeling, and it was something which I didn't dread. I felt that maybe I was dying, and I felt that if I did not get back to my body, I would be dead, gone.

Just as strikingly variable are the attitudes which different persons take to the bodies which they have left behind. It is common for a person to report feelings of concern for his body. One young woman, who was a nursing student at the time of her experience, expresses an understandable fear.

> This is sort of funny, I know, but in nursing school they had tried to drill it into us that we ought to donate our bodies to science. Well, all through this, as I watched them trying to start my breathing again, I kept thinking, "I don't want them to use that body as a cadaver."

I have heard two other person express exactly this same concern when they found themselves out of their bodies. Interestingly enough, both of them were also in the medical profession—one a physician, the other a nurse.

In another case, this concern took the form of regret. A man's heart stopped beating following a fall in which his body was badly mangled, and he recalls,

> At one time—now, I know I was lying on the bed there—but I could actually see the bed and the doctor working on me. I couldn't understand it, but I looked at my own body lying there on the bed. And I felt real bad when I looked at my body and saw how badly it was messed up.

Several persons have told me of having feelings of unfamiliarity toward their bodies, as in this rather striking passage.

> Boy, I sure didn't realize that I looked like that! You know, I'm only used to seeing myself in pictures or from the front in a mirror, and both of those look *flat*. But all of a sudden there I—or my body—was and I could see it. I could definitely see it, full view, from about five feet away. It took me a few moments to recognize myself.

In one account, this feeling of unfamiliarity took a rather extreme and humorous form. One man, a physician, tells how during his clinical "death" he was beside the bed looking at his own cadaver, which by then had turned the ash gray color assumed by bodies after death. Desperate and confused, he was trying to decide what to do. He tentatively decided just to go away, as he was feeling very uneasy. As a youngster he had been told ghost stories by his grandfather and, paradoxically, he "didn't like being around this thing that looked like a dead body—even if it was me!"

At the other extreme, some have told me that they had no particular feelings at all toward their bodies. One woman, for example, had a heart attack and felt certain she was dying. She

felt herself being pulled through darkness out of her body and
moving rapidly away. She says,

> I didn't look back at my body at all. Oh, I knew it was
> there, all right, and I could've seen it had I looked. But I
> didn't want to look, not in the least, because I knew that I
> had done my best in my life, and I was turning my atten-
> tion now to this other realm of things. I felt that to look back
> at my body would be to look back at the past, and I was
> determined not to do that.

Similarly, a girl whose out-of-body experience took place
after a wreck in which she sustained severe injuries says,

> I could see my own body all tangled up in the car
> amongst all the people who had gathered around, but, you
> know, I had no feelings for it whatsoever. It was like it was a
> completely different human, or maybe even just an object
> . . . I knew it was my body but I had no feelings for it.

Despite the eeriness of the disembodied state, the situation
has been thrust upon the dying person so suddenly that it may
take some time before the significance of what he is experiencing dawns upon him. He may be out of his body for some time,
desperately trying to sort out all the things that are happening
to him and that are racing through his mind, before he realizes
that he is dying, or even dead.

When this realization comes, it may arrive with powerful
emotional force, and provoke startling thoughts. One woman
remembers thinking, "Oh, I'm dead! How lovely!"

A man states that the thought came to him, "This must be
what they call 'death'." Even when this realization comes, it
may be accompanied by bafflement and even a certain refusal
to accept one's state. One man, for example, remembers re-
flecting upon the Biblical promise of "three score and ten"
years, and protesting that he had had "just barely one score." A
young woman gave a very impressive account of such feelings
when she told me that,

I thought I was dead, and I wasn't sorry that I was dead, but I just couldn't figure out where I was supposed to go. My thought and my consciousness were just like they are in life, but I just couldn't figure all this out. I kept thinking "Where am I going to go? What am I going to do?" and "My God, I'm dead! I can't believe it!" Because you never really believe, I don't think, fully that you're going to die. It's always something that's going to happen to the other person, and although you know it you really never believe it deep down. . . . And so I decided I was just going to wait until all the excitement died down and they carried my body away, and try to see if I could figure out where to go from there.

In one or two cases I have studied, dying persons whose souls, minds, consciousnesses (or whatever you want to label them) were released from their bodies say that they didn't feel that, after release, they were in any kind of "body" at all. They felt as though they were "pure" consciousness. One man relates that during his experience he felt as though he were "able to see everything around me—including my whole body as it lay on the bed—without occupying any space," that is, as if he were a point of consciousness. A few others say that they can't really remember whether or not they were in any kind of "body" after getting out of their physical one, because they were so taken up with the events around them.

Far and away the majority of my subjects, however, report that they did find themselves in another body upon release from the physical one. Immediately, though, we are into an area with which it is extremely difficult to deal. This "new body" is one of the two or three aspects of death experiences in which the inadequacy of human language presents the greatest obstacles. Almost everyone who has told me of this "body" has at some point become frustrated and said, "I can't describe it," or made some remark to the same effect.

Nonetheless, the accounts of this body bear a strong resemblance to one another. Thus, although different individuals use different words and draw different analogies, these varying modes of expression do seem to fall very much within the same arena. The various reports are also in very decided agreement about the general properties and characteristics of the new body. So, to adopt a term for it which will sum up its properties fairly well, and which has been used by a couple of my subjects, I shall henceforth call it the "spiritual body."

Dying persons are likely first to become aware of their spiritual bodies in the guise of their limitations. They find, when out of their physical bodies, that although they may try desperately to tell others of their plight, no one seems to hear them. This is illustrated very well in this excerpt from the story of a woman who suffered a respiratory arrest and was carried to the emergency room, where a resuscitation attempt was made.

> I saw them resuscitating me. It was really strange. I wasn't very high; it was almost like I was on a pedestal, but not above them to any great extent, just maybe looking over them. I tried talking to them but nobody could hear me, nobody would listen to me.

To complicate the fact that he is apparently inaudible to people around him, the person in a spiritual body soon finds that he is also invisible to others. The medical personnel or others congregating around his physical body may look straight towards where he is, in his spiritual body, without giving the slightest sign of ever seeing him. His spiritual body also lacks solidity; physical objects in the environment appear to move through it with ease, and he is unable to get a grip on any object or person he tries to touch.

> The doctors and nurses were pounding on my body to try to get IV's started and to get me back and I kept trying to tell them, "Leave me alone. All I want is to be left alone. Quit pounding on me." But they didn't hear me. So I tried to move their hands to keep them from beating on my body, but nothing would happen. I couldn't get anywhere. It was like—I don't really know what happened, but I couldn't move their hands. It looked like I was touching

their hands and I tried to move them—yet when I would give it the stroke, their hands were still there. I don't know whether my hand was going through it, around it, or what. I didn't feel any pressure against their hands when I was trying to move them.

Or,

People were walking up from all directions to get to the wreck. I could see them, and I was in the middle of a very narrow walkway. Anyway, as they came by they wouldn't seem to notice me. They would just keep walking with their eyes straight ahead. As they came real close, I would try to turn around, to get out of their way, but they would just walk *through* me.

Further, it is invariably reported that this spiritual body is also weightless. Most first notice this when, as in some of the excerpts given above, they find themselves floating right up to the ceiling of the room, or into the air. Many describe a "float- ing sensation," "a feeling of weightlessness," or a "drifting feeling" in association with their new bodies.

Normally, while in our physical bodies we have many modes of perception which tell us where our bodies and their various parts are in space at any given moment and whether they are moving. Vision and the sense of equilibrium are important in this respect, of course, but there is another related sense. Kinesthesia is our sense of motion or tension in our tendons, joints, and muscles. We are not usually aware of the sensations coming to us through our kinesthetic sense because our per- ception of it has become dulled through almost constant use. I suspect, however, that if it were suddenly to be cut off, one would immediately notice its absence. And, in fact, quite a few persons have commented to me that they were aware of the lack of the physical sensations of body weight, movement, and position sense while in their spiritual bodies.

These characteristics of the spiritual body which at first seem to be limitations can, with equal validity, be looked upon as the absence of limitations. Think of it this way: A person in the spiritual body is in a privileged position in relation to the other persons around him. He can see and hear them, but they can't see or hear him. (Many a spy would consider this an enviable condition.) Likewise, though the doorknob seems to go through his hand when he touches it, it really doesn't matter anyway, because he soon finds that he can just *go through* the door. Travel, once one gets the hang of it, is apparently exceptionally easy in this state. Physical objects present no barrier, and movement from one place to another can be extremely rapid, almost instantaneous.

Furthermore, despite its lack of perceptibility to people in physical bodies, all who have experienced it are in agreement that the spiritual body is nonetheless *something*, impossible to describe though it may be. It is agreed that the spiritual body has a form or shape (sometimes a globular or an amorphous cloud, but also sometimes essentially the same shape as the physical body) and even parts (projections or surfaces analogous to arms, legs, a head, etc.). Even when its shape is reported as being generally roundish in configuration, it is often said to have ends, a definite top and bottom, and even the "parts" just mentioned.

I have heard this new body described in many different terms, but one may readily see that much the same idea is being formulated in each case. Words and phrases which have been used by various subjects include a mist, a cloud, smoke-like, a vapor, transparent, a cloud of colors, wispy, an energy pattern and others which express similar meanings.

Finally, almost everyone remarks upon the *timelessness* of this out-of-body state. Many say that although they must describe their interlude in the spiritual body in temporal terms (since human language is temporal), time was not really an element of their experience as it is in physical life. Here are passages from five interviews in which some of these fantastic aspects of existence in the spiritual body are reported first-hand.

(1) I lost control of my car on a curve, and the car left the

road and went into the air, and I remember seeing the blue sky and saw that the car was going down into a ditch. At the time the car left the road, I said to myself, "I'm in an accident." At that point, I kind of lost my sense of time, and I lost my physical reality as far as my body is concerned—I lost touch with my body. My being or my self or my spirit, or whatever you would like to label it—I could sort of feel it rise out of me, out through my head. And it wasn't anything that hurt, it was just sort of like a lifting and it being above me. . . .

[My "being"] felt as if it had a *density* to it, almost, but not a physical density—kind of like, I don't know, waves or something, I guess: Nothing really physical, almost as if it were charged, if you'd like to call it that. But it felt as if it had something to it. . . . It was small, and it felt as if it were sort of circular, with no rigid outlines to it. You could liken it to a cloud. . . . It almost seemed as if it were in its own encasement. . . .

As it went out of my body, it seemed that a large end left first, and the small end last. . . . It was a very light feeling—very. There was no strain on my [physical] body; the feeling was totally separate. My body had no weight. . . .

The most striking point of the whole experience was the moment when my being was suspended above the front part of my head. It was almost like it was trying to decide whether it wanted to leave or to stay. It seemed then as though time were standing still. At the first and the last of the accident, everything moved so fast, but at this one particular time, sort of in between, as my being was suspended above me and the car was going over the embankment, it seemed that it took the car a long time to get there, and in that time I really wasn't too involved with the car or the accident or my own body—only with my mind. . . .

My being had no physical characteristics, but I have to describe it with physical terms. I could describe it in so many ways, in so many words, but none of them would be exactly right. It's so hard to describe.

Finally, the car did hit the ground and it rolled over, but my only injuries were a sprained neck and a bruised foot.

(2) [When I came out of the physical body] it was like I did come out of my body and go into something else. I didn't think I was just nothing. It was another body . . . but not another regular human body. It's a little bit different. It was not exactly like a human body, but it wasn't any big glob of matter, either. It had form to it, but no colors. And I know I still had something you could call hands.

I can't describe it. I was more fascinated with everything around me—seeing my own body there, and all—so I didn't think about the type of body I was in. And all this seemed to go so quickly. Time wasn't really an element— and yet it was. Things seem to go faster after you get out of your body.

(3) I remember being wheeled into the operating room and the next few hours were the critical period. During that time, I kept getting in and out of my physical body, and I could see it from directly above. But, while I did, I was still in a body—not a physical body, but something I can best describe as an energy pattern. If I had to put it into words, I would say that it was transparent, a spiritual as opposed to a material being. Yet, it definitely had different parts.

(4) When my heart stopped beating . . . I felt like I was a round ball and almost maybe like I might have been a little sphere—like a B-B—on the inside of this round ball. I just can't describe it to you.

(5) I was out of my body looking at it from about ten yards away, but I was still thinking, just like in physical life. And *where* I was thinking was about at my normal bodily height. I wasn't in a body, as such. I could feel something, some kind of a—like a capsule, or something, like a clear form. I couldn't really see it; it was like it was transparent,

but not really. It was like I was just there—an energy, maybe, sort of like just a little ball of energy. And I really wasn't aware of any bodily sensation—temperature, or anything like that.

In their accounts, others have briefly mentioned the likeness of shape between their physical bodies and their new ones. One woman told me that while out of her body, "I still felt an entire body form, legs, arms, everything—even while I weightless." A lady who watched the resuscitation attempt on her body from a point just below the ceiling says, "I was still in a body. I was stretched out and looking down. I moved my legs and noticed that one of them felt warmer than the other one."

Just as movement is unimpeded in this spiritual state, so, some recall, is thought. Over and over, I have been told that once they became accustomed to their new situation, people undergoing this experience began to think more lucidly and rapidly than in physical existence. For example, one man told me that while he was "dead,"

Things that are not possible now, are then. Your mind is so clear. It's so nice. My mind just took everything down and worked everything out for me the first time, without having to go through it more than once. After a while everything I was experiencing got to where it meant something to me in some way.

Perception in the new body is both like and unlike perception in the physical body. In some ways, the spiritual form is more limited. As we saw, kinesthesia, as such, in absent. In a couple of instances, persons have reported that they had no sensation of temperature, while in most cases feelings of comfortable "warmth" are reported. No one among all of my cases has reported any odors or tastes while out of their physical bodies.

On the other hand, senses which correspond to the physical senses of vision and of hearing are very definitely intact in the spiritual body, and seem actually heightened and more perfect than they are in physical life. One man says that while he was "dead" his vision seemed incredibly more powerful and, in his words, "I just can't understand how I could see so far." A woman who recalled this experience notes, "It seemed as if this spiritual sense had no limitations, as if I could look anywhere and everywhere. This phenomenon is described very graphically in this portion of an interview with a woman who was out of her body following an accident.

> There was a lot of action going on, and people running around the ambulance. And whenever I would look at a person to wonder what they were thinking, it was like a zoom-up, exactly like through a zoom lens, and I was there. But it seemed that part of me—I'll call it my mind—was still where I had been several yards away from my body. When I wanted to see someone at a distance, it seemed like part of me, kind of like a tracer, would go to that person. And it seemed to me at the time that if something happened anyplace in the world that I could just be there.

"Hearing" in the spiritual state can apparently be called so only by analogy, and most say that they do not really hear physical voices or sounds. Rather, they seem to pick up the thoughts of persons around them and, as we shall see later, this same kind of direct transfer of thoughts can play an important role in the late stages of death experiences.

As one lady put it,

> I could see people all around, and I could understand what they were saying. I didn't hear them, audibly, like I'm hearing you. It was more like knowing what they were thinking, exactly what they were thinking, but only in my mind, not in their actual vocabulary. I would catch it the second before they opened their mouths to speak.

Finally, on the basis of one unique and very interesting report, it would appear that even severe damage to the physical body in no way adversely affects the spiritual one. In this case, a man lost the better part of his leg in the accident that resulted in his clinical death. He knew this, because he saw his damaged body clearly, from a distance, as the doctor worked on it. Yet, while he was out of his body,

> I could feel my body, and it was whole. I know that. I felt whole, and I felt that all of me was there, though it wasn't.

In this disembodied state, then, a person is cut off from others. He can see other people and understand their thoughts completely, but they are able neither to see nor to hear him. Communication with other human beings is effectively cut off, even through the sense of touch, since his spiritual body lacks solidity. Thus, it is not surprising that after a time in this state profound feelings of isolation and loneliness set in. As one man put it, he could see everything around him in the hospital—all the doctors, nurses, and other personnel going about their tasks. Yet, he could not communicate with them in any way, so "I was desperately alone."

Many others have described to me the intense feelings of loneliness which overcome them at this point.

> My experience, all the things that I was going through, were so beautiful, but just indescribable. I wanted others to be there with me to see it, too, and I had the feeling that I would never be able to describe to anyone what I was seeing. I had the feeling of being lonesome because I wanted somebody to be there to experience it with me. But I knew nobody else could be there. I felt that I was in a private world at that time. I really felt a fit of depression then.

Or,

> I was unable to touch anything, unable to communicate with any of the people around. It is an awesome, lonely

feeling, a feeling of complete isolation. I knew that I was completely alone, by myself.

And again,

I was just amazed. I couldn't believe that it was happening. I wasn't really concerned or worried like "Oh, no, I'm dead and my parents are left behind and they'll be sad and I'll never see them again." Nothing like that ever entered my mind.

I was aware the whole time of being alone, though, very alone—almost like I was a visitor from someplace else. It was like all relations were cut. I know—it was like there was no love or anything. Everything was just so—technical. I don't understand, really.

The dying person's feelings of loneliness are soon dispelled, however, as he gets deeper into his near death experience. For, at some point, others come to him to give him aid in the transition he is undergoing. These may take the form of other spirits, often those of deceased relatives or friends the individual had known while he was alive. In a greater number of instances, among those I interviewed, a spiritual being of a much different character appears. In the next few sections we will look at such encounters.

Meeting Others

Quite a few have told me that at some point while they were dying—sometimes early in the experience, sometimes only after other events had taken place—they became aware of the presence of other spiritual beings in their vicinity, beings who apparently were there to ease them through their transition into death, or, in two cases, to tell them that their time to die had not yet come and that they must return to their physical bodies.

I had this experience when I was giving birth to a child. The delivery was very difficult, and I lost a lot of blood. The doctor gave me up, and told my relatives that I was dying. However, I was quite alert through the whole thing, and even as I heard him saying this I felt myself coming to. As I did, I realized that all these people were there, almost in multitudes it seems, hovering around the ceiling of the room. They were all people I had known in my past life, but who had passed on before. I recognized my grandmother and a girl I had known when I was in school, and many other relatives and friends. It seems that I mainly saw their faces and felt their presence. They all seemed pleased. It was a very happy occasion, and I felt that they had come to protect or to guide me. It was almost as if I were coming home, and they were there to greet or to welcome me. All this time, I had the feeling of everything light and beautiful. It was a beautiful and glorious moment.

One man remembers:

Several weeks before I nearly died, a good friend of mine, Bob, had been killed. Now the moment I got out of my body I had the feeling that Bob was standing there, right next to me. I could see him in my mind and felt like he was there, but it was strange. I didn't see him as his physical body. I could see things, but not in the physical form, yet just as clearly, his looks, everything. Does that make sense? He was there but he didn't have a physical body. It was kind of like a clear body, and I could sense every part of it—arms, legs, and so on—but I wasn't *seeing* it physically. I I didn't think about it being odd at the time because I didn't really need to see him with my eyes. I didn't have eyes, anyway.

I kept asking him, "Bob, where do I go now? What has happened? Am I dead or not?" And he never answered me, never said a word. But, often, while I was in the hospital, he would be there, and I would ask him again, "What's

going on?", but never any answer. And then the day the
doctors said, "He's going to live," he left. I didn't see him
again and didn't feel his presence. It was almost as though
he were waiting until I passed that final frontier and then
he would tell me, would give me the details on what was
going on.

In other cases, the spirits people encounter are not persons
whom they knew in physical life. One woman told of seeing
during her out-of-body experience not only her own transparent spiritual body but also another one, that of another person
who had died very recently. She did not know who this person
was, but made the very interesting remark that, "I did not see
this person, this spirit, as having any particular *age*, at all. I
didn't even have any sense of time myself."

In a very few instances, people have come to believe that the
beings they encountered were their "guardian spirits." One
man was told by such a spirit that, "I have helped you through
this stage of your existence, but now I am going to turn you over
to others." A woman told me that as she was leaving her body
she detected the presence of two other spiritual beings there,
and that they identified themselves as her "spiritual helpers."

In two very similar cases, persons told me of hearing a voice
which told them that they were not dead yet, but that they
must go back. As one of them tells it,

> I heard a voice, not a man's voice, but like a hearing
> beyond the physical senses, telling me what I had to
> do—go back—and I felt no fear of getting back into my
> physical body.

Finally, the spiritual beings may take a somewhat more
amorphous form.

> While I was dead, in this void, I talked to people—and
> yet, I really couldn't say that I talked to any *bodily* people.
> Yet, I had the feeling that there were people around me,
> and I could feel their presence, and could feel them mov-

ing, though I could never see anyone. Every now and then, I would talk with one of them, but I couldn't see them. And whenever I wondered what was going on, I would always get a thought back from one of them, that everything was all right, that I was dying but would be fine. So, my condition never worried me. I always got an answer back for every question that I asked. They didn't leave my mind void.

The Being Of Light

What is perhaps the most incredible common element in the accounts I have studied, and is certainly the element which has the most profound effect upon the individual, is the encounter with a very bright light. Typically, at its first appearance this light is dim, but it rapidly gets brighter until it reaches an unearthly brilliance. Yet, even though this light (usually said to be white or "clear") is of an indescribable brilliance, many make the specific point that it does not in any way hurt their eyes, or dazzle them, or keep them from seeing other things around them (perhaps because at this point they don't have physical "eyes" to be dazzled).

Despite the light's unusual manifestation, however, not one person has expressed any doubt whatsoever that it was a being, a being of light. Not only that, it is a personal being. It has a very definite personality. The love and the warmth which emanate from this being to the dying person are utterly beyond words, and he feels completely surrounded by it and taken up in it, completely at ease and accepted in the presence of this being. He senses an irresistible magnetic attraction to this light. He is ineluctably drawn to it.

Interestingly, while the above description of the being of light is utterly invariable, the identification of the being varies from individual to individual and seems to be largely a function of the religious background, training, or beliefs of the person involved. Thus, most of those who are Christians in training or belief identify the light as Christ and sometimes draw Biblical parallels in support of their interpretation. A Jewish man and woman identified the light as an "angel." It was clear, though, in both cases, that the subjects did not mean to imply that the being had wings, played a harp, or even had a human shape or appearance. There was only the light. What each was trying to get across was that they took the being to be an emissary, or a guide. A man who had had no religious beliefs or training at all prior to his experience simply identified what he saw as a "being of light." The same label was used by one lady of the Christian faith, who apparently did not feel any compulsion at all to call the light "Christ."

Shortly after its appearance, the being begins to communicate with the person who is passing over. Notably, this communication is of the same direct kind which we encountered earlier in the description of how a person in the spiritual body may "pick up the thoughts" of those around him. For, here again, people claim that they did not hear any physical voice or sounds coming from the being, nor did they respond to the being through audible sounds. Rather, it is reported that direct, unimpeded transfer of thoughts takes place, and in such a clear way that there is no possibility whatsoever either of misunderstanding or of lying to the light.

Furthermore, this unimpeded exchange does not even take place in the native language of the person. Yet, he understands perfectly and is instantaneously aware. He cannot even translate the thoughts and exchanges which took place while he was near death into the human language which he must speak now, after his resuscitation.

The next step of the experience clearly illustrates the difficulty of translating from this unspoken language. The being almost immediately directs a certain thought to the person into whose presence it has come so dramatically. Usually the persons with whom I have talked try to formulate the thought into a question. Among the translations I have heard are: "Are you prepared to die?", "Are you ready to die?", "What have you done with your life to show me?", and "What have you done with your life that is sufficient?" The first two formulations which stress "preparation," might at first seem to have a different sense from the second pair, which emphasize "accomplishment." However, some support for my own feeling that everyone is trying to express the same thought comes from the narrative of one woman who put it this way:

> The first thing he said to me was, that he kind of asked me if I was ready to die, or what I had done with my life that I wanted to show him.

Furthermore, even in the case of more unusual ways of phrasing the "question," it turns out, upon elucidation, to have much the same force. For example, one man told me that during his "death,"

> The voice asked me a question: "Is it worth it?" And what it meant was, did the kind of life I had been leading up to that point seem worthwhile to me then, knowing what I then knew.

Incidentally, all insist that this question, ultimate and profound as it may be in its emotional impact, is not at all asked in condemnation. The being, all seem to agree, does not direct the question to them to accuse or to threaten them, for they still feel the total love and acceptance coming from the light, no matter what their answer may be. Rather, the point of the question seems to be to make them think about their lives, to draw them out. It is, if you will, a Socratic question, one asked not to acquire information but to help the person who is being asked to proceed along the path to the truth by himself. Let us look at some firsthand accounts of this fantastic being.

(1) I heard the doctors say that I was dead, and that's when I began to feel as though I were tumbling, actually kind of floating, through this blackness, which was some kind of enclosure. There are not really words to describe this. Everything was very black, except that, way off from me, I could see this light. It was a very, very brilliant light,

but not too large at first. It grew larger as I came nearer and nearer to it.

I was trying to get to that light at the end, because I felt that it was Christ, and I was trying to reach that point. It was not a frightening experience. It was more or less a pleasant thing. For immediately, being a Christian, I had connected the light with Christ, who said, "I am the light of the world." I said to myself, "If this is it, if I am to die, then I know who waits for me at the end, there in that light."

(2) I got up and walked into the hall to go get a drink, and it was at that point, as they found out later, that my appendix ruptured. I became very weak, and I fell down. I began to feel a sort of drifting, a movement of my real being in and out of my body, and to hear beautiful music. I floated on down the hall and out the door onto the screened-in porch. There, it almost seemed that clouds, a pink mist really, began to gather around me, and then I floated right straight on through the screen, just as though it weren't there, and up into this pure crystal clear light, an illuminating white light. It was beautiful and so bright, so radiant, but it didn't hurt my eyes. It's not any kind of light you can describe on earth. I didn't actually see a person in this light, and yet it has a special identity, it definitely does. It is a light of perfect understanding and perfect love.

The thought came to my mind, "Lovest thou me?" This was not exactly in the form of a question, but I guess the connotation of what the light said was, "If you do love me, go back and complete what you began in your life." And all during this time, I felt as though I were surrounded by an overwhelming love and compassion.

(3) I knew I was dying and that there was nothing I could do about it, because no one could hear me. . . . I was out of my body, there's no doubt about it, because I could see my own body there on the operating room table. My soul was out! All this made me feel very bad at first, but then, this really bright light came. It did seem that it was a little dim

at first, but then it was this huge beam. It was just a tremendous amount of light, nothing like a big bright flashlight, it was just too much light. And it gave off heat to me; I felt a warm sensation.

It was a bright yellowish white—more white. It was tremendously bright; I just can't describe it. It seemed that it covered everything, yet it didn't prevent me from seeing everything around me—the operating room, the doctors and nurses, everything. I could see clearly, and it wasn't blinding.

At first, when the light came, I wasn't sure what was happening, but then, it asked, it kind of asked me if I was ready to die. It was like talking to a person, but a person wasn't there. The light's what was talking to me, but in a *voice*.

Now, I think that the voice that was talking to me actually realized that I wasn't ready to die. You know, it was just kind of testing me more than anything else. Yet, from the moment the light spoke to me, I felt really good— secure and loved. The love which came from it is just unimaginable, indescribable. It was a fun person to be with! And it had a sense of humor, too—definitely!

The Review

The initial appearance of the being of light and his probing, non-verbal questions are the prelude to a moment of startling intensity during which the being presents to the person a panoramic review of his life. It is often obvious that the being can see the individual's whole life displayed and that he doesn't himself need information. His only intention is to provoke reflection.

This review can only be described in terms of memory, since that is the closest familiar phenomenon to it, but it has characteristics which set it apart from any normal type of remembering. First of all, it is extraordinarily rapid. The memories, when they are described in temporal terms, are said to follow one another swiftly, in chronological order.

Others recall no awareness of temporal order at all. The remembrance was instantaneous; everything appeared at once, and they could take it all in with one mental glance. However it is expressed, all seem in agreement that the experience was over in an instant of earthly time.

Yet, despite its rapidity, my informants agree that the review, almost always described as a display of visual imagery, is incredibly vivid and real. In some cases, the images are reported to be in vibrant color, three-dimensional, and even moving. And even if they are flickering rapidly by, each image is perceived and recognized. Even the emotions and feelings associated with the images may be re-experienced as one is viewing them.

Some of those I interviewed claim that, while they cannot adequately explain it, everything they had ever done was there in this review—from the most insignificant to the most meaningful. Others explain that what they saw were mainly the highlights of their lives. Some have stated to me that even for a period of time following their experience of the review they could recall the events of their lives in incredible detail.

Some people characterize this as an educational effort on the part of the being of light. As they witness the display, the being seems to stress the importance of two things in life: Learning to love other people and acquiring knowledge. Let us look at a representative account of this type.

When the light appeared, the first thing he said to me was "What do you have to show me that you've done with your life?", or something to this effect. And that's when these flashbacks started. I thought, "Gee, what is going on?", because, all of a sudden, I was back early in my childhood. And from then on, it was like I was walking from the time of my very early life, on through each year of my life, right up to the present.

It was really strange where it started, too, when I was a little girl, playing down by the creek in our neighborhood, and there were other scenes from about that time—experiences I had had with my sister, and things about neighborhood people, and actual places I had been. And then I was in kindergarten, and I remembered the time when I had this one toy I really liked, and I broke it and I cried for a long time. This was a really traumatic experience for me. The images continued on through my life and I remembered when I was in Girl Scouts and went camping, and remembered many things about all the years of grammar school. Then, when I was in junior high school, it was a real big honor to be chosen for the scholastic achievement society, and I remembered when I was chosen. So, I went on through junior high, and then senior high school, and graduation, and up through my first few years of college, up to where I was then.

The things that flashed back came in the order of my life, and they were so vivid. The scenes were just like you walked ouside and saw them, completely three-dimensional, and in color. And they moved. For instance, when I saw myself breaking the toy, I could see all the movements. It wasn't like I was watching it all from my perspective at the time. It was like the little girl I saw was somebody else, in a movie, one little girl among all the other children out there playing on the playground. Yet, it was me. I saw myself doing these things, as a child, and they were the exact same things I had done, because I remember them.

Now, I didn't actually see the light as I was going through the flashbacks. He disappeared as soon as he asked me what I had done, and the flashbacks started, and yet I knew that he was there with me the whole time, that he carried me back through the flashbacks, because I felt his presence, and because he made comments here and there. He was trying to show me something in each one of these flashbacks. It's not like he was trying to see what I had done—he knew already—but he was picking out these certain flashbacks of my life and putting them in front of me so that I would have to recall them.

All through this, he kept stressing the importance of love. The places where he showed it best involved my sister; I have always been very close to her. He showed me some instances where I had been selfish to my sister, but then just as many times where I had really shown love to her and had shared with her. He pointed out to me that I should try to do things for other people, to try my best. There wasn't any accusation in any of this, though. When he came across times when I had been selfish, his attitude was only that I had been learning from them, too.

He seemed very interested in things concerning knowledge, too. He kept on pointing out things that had to do with learning, and he did say that I was going to continue learning, and he said that even when he comes back for me (because by this time he had told me that I was going back) that there will always be a quest for knowledge. He said that it is a continuous process, so I got the feeling that it goes on after death. I think that he was trying to teach me, as we went through those flashbacks.

The whole thing was really odd. I was there; I was actually seeing these flashbacks; I was actually walking through them, and it was so fast. Yet, it was slow enough that I could take it all in. Still, the time span wasn't all that large, I don't believe. It just seemed that the light came, and then I went through these flashbacks, and the light came back. It seems that it was less than five minutes, and probably more than thirty seconds, but I can't really tell you.

The only time I felt scared was when I was concerned that I wasn't going to be able to finish my life here. But I enjoyed going through this flashback. That was fun. I had a good time going back to my childhood, almost like I was reliving it. It was a way of going back and seeing it which you ordinarily just can't do.

It must also be pointed out that reports exist in which the review is experienced even though the being of light does not appear. As a rule, in experiences in which the being does apparently "direct" it, the review is a more overwhelming experience. Nonetheless, it is usually characterized as quite vivid and rapid, and as accurate, regardless of whether it occurs in the course of an actual "death" or only during a close brush with death.

After all this banging and going through this long, dark place, all of my childhood thoughts, my whole entire life was there at the end of this tunnel, just flashing in front of me. It was not exactly in terms of pictures, more in the form of thought, I guess. I can't exactly describe it to you, but it was just all there. It was just all there at once, I mean, not one thing at a time, blinking off and on, but it was everything, everything at one time. I thought about my mother, about things that I had done wrong. After I could see the mean little things I did as a child, and thought about my mother and father, I wished that I hadn't done these things, and I wished I could go back and undo them.

In the following two instances, although no clinical death had occurred at the time of the experience, actual physiological stress or injury was taking place.

The whole situation developed very suddenly. I had had a slight fever and had not felt well for about two weeks, but this night I rapidly became very ill and I felt much worse. I was lying in bed, and I remember trying to reach over to my wife and say that I was very sick, but I found it impossible to move. Beyond that, I found myself in a completely black void, and my whole life kind of flashed in front of me. It started back when I was six or seven years old, and I remembered a good friend I had in grammar school. I went from grammar school to high school to college, then to dental school, and then right on into practicing dentistry.

I knew I was dying, and I remember thinking that I wanted to provide for my family. I was distraught that I was dying and yet that there were certain things that I had done in my life that I regretted, and other things that I regretted that I had left undone.

This flashback was in the form of mental pictures, I would say, but they were much more vivid than normal ones. I saw only the high points, but it was so rapid it was like looking through a volume of my entire life and being able to do it within seconds. It just flashed before me like a motion picture that goes tremendously fast, yet I was fully able to see it, and able to comprehend it. Still, the emotions didn't come back with the pictures, because there wasn't enough time.

I didn't see anything else during this experience. There was just blackness, except for the images I saw. Yet, I definitely felt the presence of a very powerful, completely loving being there with me all through this experience.

It is really interesting. When I recovered, I could tell everyone about every part of my life, in great detail, because of what I had been through. It's quite an experience, but it's difficult to put into words, because it happens so rapidly, yet it's so clear.

A young veteran describes his review:

While I was serving in Viet Nam, I received wounds, and I later "died" from them, yet through it all I knew exactly what was going on. I was hit with six rounds of machine gun fire, and as it happened I wasn't upset at all. In my mind, I actually felt relieved when I was wounded. I felt completely at ease, and it was not frightening.

At the point of impact, my life began to become a picture in front of me, and it seemed that I could go back to the time when I was still a baby, and the pictures seemed to progress through my whole life.

I could remember everything; everything was so vivid. It was so clear in front of me. It shot right by me from the earliest things I can remember right on up to the present, and it all happened within a short time. And it was not anything bad at all; I went through it with no regrets, no derogatory feelings about myself at all.

The best thing I can think of to compare it to is a series of pictures; like slides. It was just like someone was clicking off slides in front of me, very quickly.

Finally, here is a case of an extreme emotional emergency, in which death was imminent, although no actual injuries took place.

The summer after my first year in college, I took a job driving a large semi-tractor-trailer truck. I had a problem that summer with falling asleep behind the wheel. Early one morning I was driving the truck on a long trip, and I was nodding. The last thing I remember was seeing a road sign, and then I dozed off, and the next thing I knew, I heard an awful scraping and the right outside tire blew out, and then because of the weight and sway of the truck the left tires blew out, and the truck turned over on its side and went skidding down the road towards a bridge. I was scared because I knew what was happening. I knew the truck was going to hit the bridge.

Now, during the period of time that the truck was skidding, I just thought of all the things that I had done. I only saw certain things, the high points, and it was such a real thing. The first thing I remembered was following my father as he walked along the beach; it was when I was two years old. And there were a few other things, in order, from my early years, and after that I remembered breaking my new red wagon I had gotten for Christmas when I was five. I remember crying as I went to school in the first grade, wearing that gaudy yellow raincoat my mother had bought me. I remembered a little something about each one of my years in grammar school. I remember each of my teachers, and a little something that stood out about each year. Then I went to junior high, and got a paper route, and went to work in a grocery store, and it brought me up to right then, just before beginning my second year in college.

All these things, and many others, just flashed across my mind, and it was very quick. It probably didn't last but a split second. And then it was all over and I was standing there looking at the truck, and I thought I was dead, I thought I was an angel. I started pinching myself to see if I was alive, or a ghost, or what.

The truck was a total wreck, but I didn't receive a scratch. Somehow, I had jumped out the front windshield, because all the glass was blown out. After things calmed down, I thought it was strange that these things that had happened in my life, that had made some sort of lasting impression on me, had gone through my mind during this moment of crisis. I could probably think of all those things and remember and picture each of them now, but it would probably take me at least fifteen minutes. Yet, this had all come at once, automatically, and in less than a second. It was amazing.

The Border Or Limit

In a few instances, persons have described to me how during their near-death experience they seemed to be approaching what might be called a border or a limit of some kind. This has taken the form, in various accounts, of a body of water, a gray mist, a door, a fence across a field, or simply a line. Though this is highly speculative, one could raise the question of whether there might not be some one basic experience or idea at the root of all of them. If this is true, then the different versions would merely represent varying individual ways of interpreting, wording, or remembering the root experience. Let us look at a few accounts in which the idea of a border or limit plays a prominent role.

(1) I "died" from a cardiac arrest, and, as I did, I suddenly found myself in a rolling field. It was beautiful, and

everything was an intense green—a color unlike anything on earth. There was light—beautiful, uplifting light—all around me. I looked ahead of me, across the field, and I saw a fence. I started moving towards the fence, and I saw a man on the other side of it, moving towards it as if to meet me. I wanted to reach him, but I felt myself being drawn back, irresistibly. As I did, I saw him, too, turn around and go back in the other direction, away from the fence.

(2) This experience took place during the birth of my first child. About the eighth month of my pregnancy, I developed what my doctor described as a toxic condition and advised me to enter the hospital where he could force labor. It was immediately after delivery that I had a severe hemorrhage and the doctor had a difficult time controlling it. I was aware of what was happening as, having been a nurse myself, I realized the danger. At this time, I lost consciousness, and heard an annoying buzzing, ringing sound. The next thing I knew it seemed as if I were on a ship or a small vessel sailing to the other side of a large body of water. On the distant shore, I could see all of my loved ones who had died—my mother, my father, my sister, and others. I could see them, could see their faces, just as they were when I knew them on earth. They seemed to be beckoning me to come on over, and all the while I was saying, "No, no, I'm not ready to join you. I don't want to die. I'm not ready to go."

Now, this was the strangest experience because all this time I could see all the doctors and nurses, too, as they worked on my body, but it seemed as if I were a spectator rather than that person—that body—they were working on. I was trying so hard to get through to my doctor, "I'm not going to die," but no one could hear me. Everything—the doctors, the nurses, the delivery room, the ship, the water, and the far shore—was just sort of a conglomerate. It was all together, as if one scene were superimposed right on top of the other.

Finally, the ship almost reached the far shore, but just before it did, it turned around and started back. I did finally get through to my doctor, and I was saying, "I'm not going to die." It was at this point, I guess, that I came around, and the doctor explained what had happened, that I had had a post-partum hemorrhage, and that they had nearly lost me, but that I was going to be all right.

(3) I was hospitalized for a severe kidney condition, and I was in a coma for approximately a week. My doctors were extremely uncertain as to whether I would live. During this period when I was unconscious, I felt as though I were lifted right up, just as though I didn't have a physical body at all. A brilliant white light appeared to me. The light was so bright that I could not see through it, but going into its presence was so calming and so wonderful. There is just no experience on earth like it. In the presence of the light, the thoughts or words came into my mind: "Do you want to die?" And I replied that I didn't know since I knew nothing about death. Then the white light said, "Come over this line and you will learn." I felt that I knew where the line was in front of me, although I could not actually see it. As I went across the line, the most wonderful feelings came over me—feelings of peace, tranquility, a vanishing of all worries.

(4) I had a heart attack, and I found myself in a black void, and I knew I had left my physical body behind. I knew I was dying, and I thought, "God, I did the best I knew how at the time I did it. Please help me." Immediately, I was moved out of that blackness, through a pale gray, and I just went on, gliding and moving swiftly, and in front of me, in the distance, I could see a gray mist, and I was rushing toward it. It seemed that I just couldn't get to it fast enough to satisfy me, and as I got closer to it I could see through it. Beyond the mist, I could see people, and their forms were just like they are on the earth, and I could also see something which one could

take to be buildings. The whole thing was permeated with the most gorgeous light—a living, golden yellow glow, a pale color, not like the harsh gold color we know on earth.

As I approached more closely, I felt certain that I was going through that mist. It was such a wonderful, joyous feeling; there are just no words in human language to describe it. Yet, it wasn't my time to go through the mist, because instantly from the other side appeared my Uncle Carl, who had died many years earlier. He blocked my path, saying, "Go back. Your work on earth has not been completed. Go back now." I didn't want to go back, but I had no choice, and immediately I was back in my body. I felt that horrible pain in my chest, and I heard my little boy crying, "God, bring my mommy back to me."

(5) I was taken to the hospital for a critical condition they said was an "inflammation" and my doctor said I wasn't going to make it. He told my relatives to come because I wasn't going to be here much longer. They came, and gathered around my bed, and as the doctor thought I was dying, my relatives looked like they were going farther away from me. It looked like they were going back instead of me going away from them. It got dimmer and dimmer, but I saw them. I lost consciousness and didn't seem to know anything else about what was going on in the hospital room, but I was in a narrow, v-shaped passage, like a trough, about the width of this chair. It just fit my body, and my hands and arms seemed to be down at my side. I went head first, and it was dark, dark as it could be in there. I moved on through it, downward, and I looked up and saw a beautiful, polished door, with no knob. Around the edges of the door I could see a really brilliant light, with rays just streaming like everybody was so happy in there, and reeling around, moving around. It seemed like it was awfully busy in there. I looked up and said, "Lord, here I am. If you want me, take me." Boy, he shot me back so fast it felt like I almost lost my breath.

Coming Back

Obviously, all the persons with whom I have talked had to "come back" at some point in their experience. Usually, though, an interesting change in their attitude had taken place by this time. Remember that the most common feelings reported in the first few moments following death are a desperate desire to get back into the body and an intense regret over one's demise. However, once the dying person reaches a certain depth in his experience, he does not want to come back, and he may even resist the return to the body. This is especially the case for those who have gotten so far as to encounter the being of light. As one man put it, most emphatically, "I *never* wanted to leave the presence of this being."

Exceptions to this generalization are often only apparent, not real. Several women who were mothers of young children at the time of their experience have told me that, while for *themselves* they would have preferred to stay where they were, they felt an obligation to try to go back and to raise their children.

I wondered whether I should stay there, but as I did I remembered my family, my three children and my husband. Now, this is the part that is hard to get across: When I had this wonderful feeling, there in the presence of that light, I really didn't want to come back. But I take my responsibilities very seriously, and I knew that I had a duty to my family. So I decided to try to come back.

In several other cases, persons have told me that, though they were comfortable and secure in their new disembodied existence and were even enjoying it, they felt happy to be able to return to physical life since they had left some important task undone. In a few cases, this has taken the form of a desire to complete an unfinished education.

I had completed three years of college and had only one more year to go. I kept thinking, "I don't want to die now." But I feel that if this had gone on just a few minutes more, if I had been with this light for just a little while longer, I wouldn't have thought of my education anymore, that I would've been taken up with the other things I was experiencing.

The accounts I have collected present an extremely varied picture when it comes to the question of the mode of return to physical life and of why the return took place. Most say simply that they do not know how or why they returned, or that they can only make guesses. A few very definitely feel that their own decisions to get back to the body and to return to earthly life were the operative factors.

I was out of my body, and I realized that I had to make a decision. I knew that I could not stay out of my physical body for a very long period of time so—well, for others this is very hard to understand, but for me then it was perfectly clear—I knew that I had to decide whether to move on out or to get back in.

It was wonderful over there on the other side, and I kind of wanted to stay. But knowing that I had something good to do on earth was just as wonderful in a way. So, I was thinking, "Yes, I must go back and live," and I got back into my physical body. I almost feel as though I stopped the bleeding myself. At any rate, I began to recover after that.

Others feel that they were in effect *allowed* to live by "God," or by the being of light, either in response to their own request to be allowed to live (usually because the request was made unselfishly) or because God or the being apparently had some mission in mind for them to fulfill.

I was above the table, and I could see everything they were doing. I knew that I was dying, that this would be it. Yet, I was concerned about my children, about who would take care of them. So, I was not ready to go. The Lord permitted me to live.

As one man remembers,

I say God surely was good to me, because I was dead, and he let the doctors bring me back, for a purpose. The purpose was to help my wife, I think, because she had a drinking problem, and I know that she just couldn't have made it without me. She is better now, though, and I really think it had a lot to do with what I went through.

A young mother feels that,

The Lord sent me back, but I don't know why. I definitely felt Him there, and knew that He recognized me and knew who I was. And yet He didn't see fit to let me into heaven; but why, I don't know. I have thought about it many times since, and I believe that it was either because I had those two small children to raise, or because I personally just wasn't ready to be there. I am still seeking the answer, and I just can't figure it out.

In a few instances, persons have expressed the feeling that the love or prayers of others have in effect pulled them back from death regardless of their own wishes.

I was with my elderly aunt during her last illness, which was very drawn out. I helped take care of her, and all that time everyone in the family was praying for her to regain her health. She stopped breathing several times, but they brought her back. Finally, one day she looked at me and she said, "Joan, I have been over there, over to the beyond and it is beautiful over there. I want to stay, but I can't as long as you keep praying for me to stay with you. Your prayers are holding me over here. Please don't pray any more." We did all stop, and shortly after that she died.

A woman told me,

> The doctor had already said that I was gone, but I lived through it. Yet, the experience I had been through was so joyous, I had no bad feelings at all. As I came back, I opened my eyes, and my sister and my husband saw me. I could see their relief, and tears were pouring from their eyes. I could see that it was a relief to them that I did survive. I felt as though I had been called back— magnetized back—through the love of my sister and my husband. Since then, I have believed that other people can draw you back.

In quite a few instances, persons recall being drawn rapidly back through the dark tunnel through which they went during the initial moments of their experience. One man who died, for example, relates how he was propelled forward through a dark valley. He felt he was approaching the end of the tunnel, yet just at that moment he heard his name called from behind. He then was drawn backwards through the same space.

Few experience the actual re-entry into their physical bodies. Most report that they simply felt that at the end of their experience they "went to sleep" or lapsed into unconsciousness, later to awaken in their physical bodies.

> I don't remember getting back into my body. It was like I just drifted away, went to sleep, and then all of a sudden I woke right back up and I was lying in the bed. The people in the room were, in comparison, where they had been while I had been out of my body, looking at it and at them.

On the other hand, some remember being drawn speedily back towards their physical bodies, often with a jerk, at the end of their experiences.

> I was up there at the ceiling, watching them work on me. When they put the shocks on my chest, and my body jumped up, I just fell right back down to my body, just like

dead weight. The next thing I knew, I was in my body again.

And

And I decided that I would come back, and when I did, it was like a jolt, like a jolt back into my body, and I felt that at that very moment I crossed back over into life.

In the very few accounts in which the event is recalled in some detail, re-entry is said to occur "through the head."

My "being" seemed to have a small end and a large end, and at the end of my accident, after it had just hung suspended over my head, it came back in. When it left my body, it seemed that the large end left first, but coming back in, the small end seemed to come in first.

One person recounted:

When I saw them pick up my body and take it out from under the steering wheel, it was just like a swoooosh and I felt like I was drawn through a limited area, a kind of funnel, I guess. It was dark and black in there, and I moved through it quickly, back to my body. And as I was being sucked back, it seemed that the suction started from the head, like I went into the head. I didn't feel that I had any say-so about it at all, nor even any time to think about it. I was there, yards away from my body, and all of a sudden, it was over with. I didn't even have time to think, "I'm being sucked back into my body."

Typically, the moods and feelings which were associated with the experience linger on for some time after the actual medical crisis has been resolved.

(1) After I came back, I cried off and on for about a week because I had to live in this world after seeing that one. I didn't want to come back.

(2) When I came back, I brought with me some of the wonderful feelings I had over there. They lasted for several days. Even now I feel them sometimes.

(3) This feeling was so indescribable. It has stayed with me, in a way. I've never forgotten it. I still think about it very often.

Telling Others

It must be emphasized that a person who has been through an experience of this type has no doubt whatsoever as to its reality and its importance. Interviews which I have done are usually sprinkled with remarks to precisely that effect. For example:

While I was out of my body, I was really amazed at what was happening to me. I couldn't understand it. But it was real. I saw my body so plainly, and from so far away. My mind wasn't at that point where I wanted to make things happen or make up anything. My mind wasn't manufacturing ideas. I just wasn't in that state of mind.

And

It was nothing like an hallucination. I have had hallucinations once, when I was given codeine in the hospital. But that had happened long before the accident which really killed me. And this experience was nothing like the hallucinations, nothing like them at all.

Such remarks come from persons who are very capable of distinguishing dream and fantasy from reality. The people I have interviewed are functional, well-balanced personalities. Yet, they do not tell their experiences as they would dreams, but rather as real events which actually happened to them.

Despite their own certainty of the reality and importance of what has happened to them, they realize that our contemporary society is just not the sort of environment in which reports

of this nature would be received with sympathy and understanding. Indeed, many have remarked that they realized from
the very beginning that others would think they were mentally
unstable if they were to relate their experiences. So, they have
resolved to remain silent on the subject or else to reveal their
experiences only to some very close relative.

> It was very interesting. It's just that I don't like telling
> people about it. People just kind of look at you like you're
> crazy.

Another recalls,

> I didn't tell anyone about it for a long, long time. I just
> didn't say anything at all about it. I felt funny about it
> because I was afraid that nobody would think I was telling
> the truth, that they would say, "Oh, you're making up these
> things."
> One day, I decided, "Well, I'll see how my family reacts
> to it," and I told them, but never anyone else until now.
> But I think that my family realized that I had been that far.

Others tried at first to tell someone else, but were rebuffed,
so they resolved from then on to remain silent.

> (1) The only person I tried to tell was my mother. Just a
> little later I mentioned to her how I had felt. But I was just
> a little boy, and she didn't pay any attention to me. So I
> never told it to anybody else.

> (2) I tried to tell my minister, but he told me I had been
> hallucinating, so I shut up.

> (3) I was pretty popular in junior high and high school,
> and I just floated with the crowd, never anything new. I
> was a follower, not a leader. And after this happened to me,
> and I tried to tell people, they just automatically labeled
> me as crazy, I think. I would try to tell people this, and they

would listen with interest, but then I would find out later that they'd go say, "She has really flipped out." When I saw that it was just a big joke, I quit trying to communicate about it. I hadn't been trying to get across the idea that, "Gee, this strange experience has happened to me." What I was trying to say was that there was more we needed to know about life than I had ever thought about, and I am sure they hadn't either.

(4) I tried to tell my nurses what had happened when I woke up, but they told me not to talk about it, that I was just imagining things.

So, in the words of one person,

You learn very quickly that people don't take to this as easily as you would like for them to. You simply don't jump up on a little soapbox and go around telling everyone these things.

Interestingly enough, in only one of the cases I have studied did a physician reveal any familiarity at all with near-death experiences or express any sympathy with them. After her out-of-body experience, one girl told me,

My family and I asked the doctor about what had happened to me, and he said that this happened a lot when a person is in severe pain or has severe injuries, that their soul will leave their body.

Considering the skepticism and lack of understanding that greet the attempt of a person to discuss his near-death experience, it is not surprising that almost everyone in this situation comes to feel that he is unique, that no one else has ever undergone what he has. For example, one man told me, "I have been somewhere nobody else has ever been."

It has often happened that when, after first interviewing someone in detail about his own experience, I have proceeded to tell him that others have reported exactly the same events and perceptions, he has expressed profound feelings of relief.

It is a very interesting thing to find out that other people have had the same experience, because I hadn't realized. . . . I am actually happy that I have heard this, knowing that obviously someone else has been through this, too. Now I *know* I'm not crazy.

It was always such a real thing to me, but I never would tell anybody because I was scared that they would look at me and think, "When you arrested, your mind went bad at the same time!"

I figured that someone else would've had this same experience, but that I probably never would meet up with anybody who knew another person who had, because I don't think people are going to talk. If somebody were to come up and tell me, without me ever having been there, I would probably look at them and wonder what they were trying to pull over on me, because that's just the way our society is.

There is yet another reason why some are reticent to relate their experiences to others. They feel that the experience is so indescribable, so far beyond human language and human modes of perception and existence, that it is fruitless even to try.

Effects On Lives

For the reasons just explained, no one in my experience has built himself a portable lectern and gone out to preach about his experience on a full time basis. No one has seen fit to proselytize, to try to convince others of the realities he experienced. Indeed, I have found that the difficulty is quite the reverse: People are naturally very reticent to tell others about what happened to them.

The effects which their experiences have had on their lives

seem to have taken subtler, quieter forms. Many have told me that they felt that their lives were broadened and deepened by their experience, that because of it they became more reflective and more concerned with ultimate philosophical issues.

At this time—it was before I had gone off to college—I had grown up in a very small town, with very small-minded people, the people I was associated with, anyway. I was a typical high school fraternity brat. You just weren't "it" unless you belonged to my fraternity.

But after this thing happened to me, I wanted to know more. At the time, though, I didn't think there was a person who would know anything about this, because I had never been out of this little world that I was in. I didn't know anything about psychology, or anything like that. All I knew was that I felt like I had aged overnight after this happened, because it opened up a whole new world for me that I never knew could possibly exist. I kept thinking, "There's so much that I've got to find out." In other words, there's more to life than Friday night movies and the football game. And there's more to me that I don't even know about. And then I started thinking about "What is the limit of the human and of the mind?" It just opened me up to a whole new world.

Another states,

Since then, it has been on my mind constantly what I have done with my life, and what I will do with my life. My past life—I'm satisfied with it. I don't think the world owes me anything because I really did everything I wanted and I did it the way I wanted to, and I'm still alive and I can do some more. But since I died, all of a sudden, right after my experience, I started wondering whether I had been doing the things I had done because they were good, or because they were good for *me*. Before, I just reacted off the impulse, and now I run things through my mind first, nice and slow. Everything seems to have to go through my mind and be digested, first.

I try to do things that have more meaning, and that makes my mind and soul feel better. And I try not to be biased, and not to judge people. I want to do things because they are good, not because they are good to me. And it seems that the understanding I have of things now is so much better. I feel like this is because of what happened to me, because of the places I went and the things I saw in this experience.

Others report a changed attitude or approach towards the physical life to which they have returned. One woman, for instance, says quite simply that "it made life much more precious to me."
Another person relates how,

It was a blessing in a way, because before that heart attack I was too busy planning for my children's future, and worrying about yesterday, that I was losing the joys of the present. I have a much different attitude now.

A few have mentioned that what they underwent changed their concepts of the mind and of the relative importance of the physical body as against the mind. This is illustrated especially well in these words of a woman who had an out-of-body experience while near death.

I was more conscious of my mind at the time than of that physical body. The mind was the most important part, instead of the shape of the body. And before, all my life, it had been exactly reversed. The body was my main interest and what was going on in my mind, well, it was just going on, and that's all. But after this happened, my mind was the main point of attraction, and the body was second—it was only something to encase my mind. I didn't care if I had a body or not. It didn't matter because for all I cared my mind was what was important.

In a very small number of cases, persons have told me that after their experiences they seemed to acquire or to notice faculties of intuition bordering on the psychic.

(1) Following this experience, it almost seemed as if I were filled with a new spirit. Since then, many have remarked to me that I seem to have almost a calming effect on them, instantly, when they are troubled. And it seems that I am more in tune with people now, that I can pick up things about them faster.

(2) One thing that I think has been given to me, because of my death experience, is that I can sense the needs in other individuals' lives. Often, for instance when I have been with people on the elevator in the office building where I work, it seems I can almost read their faces, and tell that they need help, and what kind. Many times, I have spoken to people who are troubled like this, and have led them into my office for counseling.

(3) Since I was hurt, I've had the feeling of picking up people's thoughts and vibrations, and I can feel resentment from other people. I have often been able to pick up what people were going to say before they said it. Not many people will believe me, but I've had some really odd, odd experiences since then. One time, I was at a party and was picking up other people's thoughts, and some people there who didn't know me got up and left. They were scared that I was a witch or something. I don't know if it is something I picked up while I was dead, or if it was there dormant and I never did use it until after this happened.

There is a remarkable agreement in the "lessons," as it were, which have been brought back from these close encounters with death. Almost everyone has stressed the importance in this life of trying to cultivate love for others, a love of a unique and profound kind. One man who met the being of light felt totally loved and accepted, even while his whole life was displayed in a panorama for the being to see. He felt that the "question" that the being was asking him was whether he was able to love others in the same way. He now feels that it is his commission while on earth to try to learn to be able to do so.

In addition, many others have emphasized the importance of seeking knowledge. During their experiences, it was intimated to them that the acquisition of knowledge continues even in the after-life. One woman, for example, has taken advantage of every educational opportunity she has had since her "death" experience. Another man offers the advice, "No matter how old you are, don't stop learning. For this is a process, I gather, that goes on for eternity."

No one that I interviewed has reported coming out of this experience feeling morally "purified" or perfected. No one with whom I have talked in any way evinces a "holier-than-thou" attitude. In fact, most have specifically brought up the point that they feel that they are still trying, still searching. Their vision left them with new goals, new moral principles, and a renewed determination to try to live in accordance with them, but with no feelings of instantaneous salvation or of moral infallibility.

New Views of Death

As one might reasonably expect, this experience has a profound effect upon one's attitude towards physical death, especially for those who had not previously expected that anything took place after death. In some form or another, almost every person has expressed to me the thought that he is no longer afraid of death. This requires clarification, though. In the first place, certain modes of death are obviously undesirable, and secondly, none of these persons are actively seeking death. They all feel that they have tasks to do as long as they are physically alive and would agree with the words of a man who told me, "I've got quite a lot of changing to do before I leave here." Likewise, all would disavow suicide as a means by which to return to the realms they glimpsed during their experiences.

It is just that now the state of death itself is no longer forbidding to them. Let us look at some passages in which such attitudes are explained.

(1) I suppose this experience molded something in my life. I was only a child when it happened, only ten, but now, my entire life through, I am thoroughly convinced that there is life after death, without a shadow of a doubt, and I am not afraid to die. I am not. Some people I have known are so afraid, so scared. I always smile to myself when I hear people doubt that there is an afterlife, or say, "When you're dead, you're gone." I think to myself, "They really don't know."

I've had many things happen to me in my life. In business, I've had a gun pulled on me and put to my temple. And it didn't frighten me very much, because I thought, "Well, if I really die, if they really kill me, I know I'll still live somewhere."

(2) When I was a little boy I used to dread dying. I used to wake up at night crying and having a fit. My mother and father would rush into the bedroom and ask what was wrong. I told them that I didn't want to die, but that I knew I had to, and asked if they could stop it. My mother would talk to me and tell me, "No, that's just the way it is and we all have to face it." She said that we all had to do it alone and that when the time came we would do it all right. And years later after my mother died I would talk about death with my wife. I still feared it. I didn't want it to come.

But since this experience, I don't fear death. Those feelings vanished. I don't feel bad at funerals anymore. I kind of rejoice at them, because I know what the dead person has been through.

I believe that the Lord may have sent this experience to me because of the way I felt about death. Of course, my parents comforted me, but the Lord *showed* me, whereas they couldn't do that. Now, I don't talk about all this, but I know, and I am perfectly satisfied.

(3) Now, I am not afraid to die. It's not that I have a death wish, or want to die right now. I don't want to be living over there on the other side now, because I'm supposed to be living here. The reason why I'm not afraid to die, though, is that I know where I'm going when I leave here, because I've been there before.

(4) The last thing the light said to me, before I came back to my body, back to life, was—well, what it boiled down to was that he would be back. He was telling me that I was going to go on and live this time, but that there would be a time when he would be getting in touch with me again, and that I would actually die.

So I know that the light will come back, and the voice, but as to when, I'm not sure. I think that it'll be a very similar experience, but I think a better one, really, since now I know what to expect and won't be so confused. I don't think I want to go back anytime soon, though. I still want to do some things down here.

The reason why death is no longer frightening, as all of these excerpts express, is that after his experience a person no longer entertains any doubts about his survival of bodily death. It is no longer merely an abstract possibility to him, but a fact of his experience.

Remember that much earlier I discussed the "annihilation" concept, which uses "sleeping" and "forgetting" as its models of death. Persons who have "died" disavow models like this and choose analogies which portray death as a transition from one state to another, or as an entry into a higher state of consciousness or of being. One woman, whose deceased relatives were there to greet her at her death, compared death to a "homecoming." Others have likened it to other psychologically positive states, for example, to awakening, to graduating, and to escape from jail.

(1) Some say that we are not using the word "death" because we are trying to escape from it. That's not true in

my case. After you've once had the experience that I had, you know in your heart that there's no such thing as death. You just graduate from one thing to another—like from grammar school to high school to college.

(2) Life is like imprisonment. In this state, we just can't understand what prisons these bodies are. Death is such a release—like an escape from prison. That's the best thing I can think of to compare it to.

Even those who previously had some traditional conviction about the nature of the afterlife world seem to have moved away from it to some degree following their own brushes with death. In fact, in all the reports I have gathered, not one person has painted the mythological picture of what lies hereafter. No one has described the cartoonist's heaven of pearly gates, golden streets, and winged, harp-playing angels, nor a hell of flames and demons with pitchforks.

So, in most cases, the reward-punishment model of the afterlife is abandoned and disavowed, even by many who had been accustomed to thinking in those terms. They found, much to their amazement, that even when their most apparently awful and sinful deeds were made manifest before the being of light, the being responded not with anger and rage, but rather only with understanding, and even with humor. As one woman went through the review of her life with this being, she saw some scenes in which she had failed to show love and had shown selfishness. Yet, she says, "His attitude when we came to these scenes was just that I had been learning, even then." In place of this old model, many seemed to have returned with a new model and a new understanding of the world beyond—a vision which features not unilateral judgement, but rather cooperative development towards the ultimate end of self-realization. According to these new views, development of the soul, especially in the spiritual faculties of love and knowledge, does not stop upon death. Rather, it continues on the other side, perhaps eternally, but certainly for a period of time and to a depth which can only be glimpsed, while we are still in physical bodies, "through a glass, darkly."

Corroboration

The question naturally arises whether any evidence of the reality of near-death experiences might be acquired independently of the descriptions of the experiences themselves. Many persons report being out of their bodies for extended periods and witnessing many events in the physical world during the interlude. Can any of these reports be checked out with other witnesses who were known to be present, or with later confirming events, and thus be corroborated?

In quite a few instances, the somewhat surprising answer to this question is, "yes." Furthermore, the description of events witnessed while out of the body tend to check out fairly well. Several doctors have told me, for example, that they are utterly baffled about how patients with no medical knowledge could describe in such detail and so correctly the procedure used in resuscitation attempts, even though these events took place while the doctors knew the patients involved to be "dead."

In several cases, persons have related to me how they amazed their doctors or others with reports of events they had witnessed while out of the body. While she was dying, for example, one girl went out of her body and into another room in the hospital where she found her older sister crying and saying, "Oh, Kathy, please don't die, please don't die." The older sister was quite baffled when, later, Kathy told her exactly where she had been and what she had been saying, during this time. In the two passages which follow, similar events are described.

(1) After it was all over, the doctor told me that I had a really bad time, and I said, "Yeah, I know." He said, "Well, how do you know?" and I said, "I can tell you everything that happened." He didn't believe me, so I told him the whole story, from the time I stopped breathing until the

time I was kind of coming around. He was really shocked to know that I knew everything that had happened. He didn't know quite what to say, but he came in several times to ask me different things about it.

(2) When I woke up after the accident, my father was there, and I didn't even want to know what sort of shape I was in, or how I was, or how the doctors thought I would be. All I wanted to talk about was the experience I had been through. I told my father who had dragged my body out of the building, and even what color clothes that person had on, and how they got me out, and even about all the conversation that had been going on in the area. And my father said, "Well, yes, these things were true." Yet, my body was physically out this whole time, and there was no way I could have seen or heard these things without being outside of my body.

Finally, in a few cases, I have been able to get the independent testimony of others about corroborating events. In assessing the evidential value of such independent reports, however, several complicating factors arise. First, in most of the cases the corroborating event itself is attested to only by the dying person himself and by at most a couple of close friends and acquaintances. Second, even in the exceptionally dramatic, well-attested instances I have collected, I have promised not to reveal actual names. Even if I could, though, I do not think that such corroborating stories collected after the fact would constitute *proof*, for reasons which I shall explain in the final chapter.

We have reached the end of our survey of the various commonly-reported stages and events of the experience of dying. In closing this chapter, I want to quote at some length from a rather exceptional account which embodies many of the elements I have discussed. In addition, however, it contains a unique twist not encountered before: The being of light tells the man involved of his impending death in advance, and then decides subsequently to let him live.

At the time this happened I suffered, as I still do, with a very severe case of bronchial asthma and emphysema. One day, I got into a coughing fit and apparently ruptured a disk in the lower part of my spine. For a couple of months, I consulted a number of doctors for the agonizing pain, and finally one of them referred me to a neurosurgeon, Dr. Wyatt. He saw me and told me that I needed to be admitted to the hospital immediately, so I went on in and they put me in traction right away.

Dr. Wyatt knew that I had bad respiratory diseases so he called in a lung specialist, who said that the anesthesiologist, Dr. Coleman, should be consulted if I was going to be put to sleep. So the lung specialist worked on me for almost three weeks until he finally got me to a place where Dr. Coleman would put me under. He finally consented on a Monday, although he was very much worried about it. They scheduled the operation for the next Friday. Monday night, I went to sleep and had a restful sleep until sometime early Tuesday morning, when I woke up in severe pain. I turned over and tried to get in a more comfortable position, but just at that moment a light appeared in the corner of the room, just below the ceiling. It was just a ball of light, almost like a globe, and it was not very large, I would say no more than twelve to fifteen inches in diameter, and as this light appeared, a feeling came over me. I can't say that it was an eerie feeling, because it was not. It was a feeling of complete peace and utter relaxation. I could see a hand reach down for me from the light, and the light said, "Come with me. I want to show you something." So immediately, without any hesitation whatsoever, I reached up with my hand and grabbed onto the hand I saw. As I did, I had the feeling of being drawn up and of leaving my body, and I looked back and saw it lying there on the bed while I was going up towards the ceiling of the room.

Now, at this time, as soon as I left my body, I took on the same form as the light. I got the feeling, and I'll have to use my own words for it, because I've never heard anyone talk about anything like this, that this form was definitely a spirit. It wasn't a body, just a wisp of smoke or a vapor. It looked almost like the clouds of cigarette smoke you can see when they are illuminated as they drift around a lamp. The form I took had colors, though. There was orange, yellow, and a color that was very indistinct to me—I took it to be an indigo, a bluish color.

This spiritual form didn't have a shape like a body. It was more or less circular, but it had what I would call a hand. I know this because when the light reached down for me, I reached up for it with my hand. Yet, the arm and hand of my body just stayed put, because I could see them lying on the bed, down by the side of my body, as I rose up to the light. But when I wasn't using this spiritual hand, the spirit went back to the circular pattern.

So, I was drawn up to the same position the light was in, and we started moving through the ceiling and the wall of the hospital room, into the corridor, and through the corridor, down through the floors it seemed, on down to a lower floor in the hospital. We had no difficulty in passing through doors or walls. They would just fade away from us as we would approach them.

During this period it seemed that we were traveling. I knew we were moving, yet there was no sensation of speed. And in a moment, almost instantaneously, really, I realized that we had reached the recovery room of the hospital. Now, I hadn't even known where the recovery room was at this hospital, but we got there, and again, we were in the corner of the room near the ceiling, up above everything else. I saw the doctors and nurses walking around in their green suits and saw the beds that were placed around in there.

This being then told me—he showed me—"That's where you're going to be. When they bring you off the operating table they're going to put you in that bed, but you will never awaken from that position. You'll know nothing after you go to the operating room until I come back to get you sometime after this." Now, I won't say this was in words. It wasn't like an audible voice, because if it had been I would have expected the others in the room to have heard the voice, and they didn't. It was more of an impression that came to me. But it was in such a vivid form that there was no way for me to say I didn't hear it or I didn't feel it. It was definite to me.

And what I was seeing—well, it was so much easier to recognize things while I was in this spiritual form. I was now wondering, like, "Now, what is that that he is trying to show me." I knew immediately what it was, what he had in mind. There was no doubt. It was that *that bed*—it was the bed on the right just as you come in from the corridor—is where I'm going to be and he's brought me here for a purpose. And then he told me why. It came to me that the reason for this was that he didn't want any fear when the time came that my spirit passed from my body, but that he wanted me to know what the sensation would be on passing that point. He wanted to assure me so that I wouldn't be afraid, because he was telling me that he wouldn't be there immediately that I would go through other things first, but that he would be overshadowing everything that happened and would be there for me at the end.

Now, immediately, when I had joined him to take the trip to the recovery room and had become a spirit myself, in a way we had been fused into one. We were two separate ones, too, of course. Yet, he had full control of everything that was going on as far as I was concerned. And even if we were traveling through the walls and ceilings and so forth, well, it just seemed that we were in such close communication that nothing whatsoever could have bothered me. Again, it was just a peacefulness, calmness, and a serenity that have never been found anywhere else.

So, after he told me this, he took me back to my hospital room, and as I got back I saw my body again, still lying in the same position as when we left, and instantaneously I was back in my body. I would guess that I had been out of my body for five or ten minutes, but passage of time had nothing to do with this experience. In fact, I don't remember if I have ever even thought of it as being any particular time.

Now, this whole thing had just astounded me, took me completely by surprise. It was so vivid and real—more so than ordinary experience. And the next morning, I was not in the least afraid. When I shaved, I noticed that my hand didn't shake like it had been doing for six or eight weeks before then. I knew that I would be dying, and there was no regret, no fear. There was no thought, "What can I do to keep this from happening?" I was ready.

Now, on Thursday afternoon, the day before the operation the next morning, I was in my hospital room, and I was worried. My wife and I have a boy, an adopted nephew, and we were then having some trouble with him. So I decided to write a letter to my wife and one to my nephew, putting some of my worries in words, and to hide the letters where they wouldn't be found until after the operation. After I had written about two pages of the letter to my wife, it was just as if the floodgates had opened. All at once, I broke out in tears, sobbing. I felt a presence, and at first I thought maybe that I had cried so loud that I had disturbed one of the nurses, and that they had come in to see what was the matter with me. But I hadn't heard the door open. And again I felt this presence, but I didn't see any light this time, and thoughts or words came to me, just as before, and he said, "Jack, why are you crying? I thought you would be pleased to be with me." I thought, "Yes, I am. I want to go very much." And the voice said, "Then why are you crying?" I said, "We've had trouble with our nephew, you know, and I'm afraid my wife won't know how to raise him. I'm trying to put into words how I feel, and what I want her to try to do for him. I'm concerned, too, because I feel that maybe my presence could have settled him down some."

Then the thoughts came to me, from this presence,

"Since you are asking for someone else, and thinking of others, not Jack, I will grant what you want. You will live until you see your nephew become a man." And just like that, it was gone. I stopped crying, and I destroyed the letter so my wife wouldn't accidentally find it.

That evening, Dr. Coleman came in and told me that he was expecting a lot of trouble with putting me to sleep, and for me not to be surprised to wake up and find a lot of wires and tubes and machines all around me. I didn't tell him what I had experienced, so I just nodded and said I would cooperate.

The next morning the operation took a long time but went fine, and as I was regaining my consciousness, Dr. Coleman was there with me, and I told him, "I know exactly where I am." He asked, "What bed are you in?" I said, "I'm in that first bed on the right just as you come in from the hall." He just kind of laughed, and of course, he thought I was just talking from the anesthetic.

I wanted to tell him what had happened, but just in a moment Dr. Wyatt came in and said, "He's awake now. What do you want to do?" And Dr. Coleman said, "There's not a thing I can do. I've never been so amazed in my life. Here I am with all this equipment set up and he doesn't need a thing." Dr. Wyatt said, "Miracles still happen, you know." So, when I could get up in the bed, and see around the room, I saw that I was in that same bed that the light had shown me several days before.

Now, all this was three years ago, but it is still just as vivid as it was then. It was the most fantastic thing that has ever happened to me, and it has made a big difference. But I don't talk about it. I have only told my wife, my brother, my minister, and now you. I don't know how to say it, but this is so hard to explain. I'm not trying to make a big explosion in your life, and I'm not trying to brag. It's just that after this, I don't have any doubts anymore. I know there is life after death.

III.
PARALLELS

T he events of the various stages of the experience of dying are, to say the very least, unusual. Hence, my surprise has been compounded as over the years I have come across quite a number of striking parallels to them. These parallels occur in ancient and/or highly esoteric writings from the literature of several very diverse civilizations, cultures, and eras.

The Bible

In our society *The Bible* is the most widely read and discussed book dealing with matters relating to the nature of the spiritual aspect of man and to life after death. On the whole, however, *The Bible* has relatively little to say about the events that transpire upon death, or about the precise nature of the after-death world. This is especially true of the *Old Testament*. According to some Biblical scholars, only two passages in all of the *Old Testament* speak unequivocally of life after death:

> Isaiah 26:19: Thy dead men shall live, together with my dead body shall they arise. Awake and sing, ye that dwell in dust for . . . the earth shall cast out the dead.[1]

> Daniel 12:2: And many of them that sleep in the dust of the earth shall awake, some to everlasting life, and some to shame and everlasting contempt.

Notice that in both of these passages there is the strong suggestion that a resurrection of the physical body will occur and that the state of physical death is compared here, again, to sleep.

Still, as is evident from the preceding chapter, a few persons have drawn upon specific Biblical concepts when trying to elucidate or to explain to me what happened to them. For instance, it will be remembered that one man identified the dark enclosure he went through at the moment of death as the Biblical "valley of the shadow of death." Two persons mentioned Jesus' claim, "I am the light of the world." Apparently, it was at least partly on the basis of that phrase that both identified the light they met as Christ. One of them told me, "I didn't ever see a person in this light, but to me the light was a Christ—consciousness, a oneness with all things, a perfect love. I think that Jesus meant it literally when he said he was the light of the world."

In addition, in my own reading I have come across a few seeming parallels which none of my subjects have mentioned. The most interesting ones occur in the writings of the apostle Paul. He was a persecutor of Christians until he had his famous vision and conversion on the road to Damascus. He says:

> Acts 26:13-26: At midday, O king, I saw in the way a light from heaven, above the brightness of the sun, shining

round about me and them which journeyed with me. And when we were all fallen to the earth, I heard a voice speaking unto me, and saying in the Hebrew tongue, "Saul, Saul, why persecutest thou me? It is hard for thee to kick against the pricks."

And I said, "Who art thou, Lord?" And he said, "I am Jesus, whom thou persecutest. But rise, and stand upon thy feet: for I have appeared unto thee for this purpose, to make thee a minister and a witness, both of these things which thou hast seen, and of those things in which I will appear unto thee. . . ."

Whereupon, O King Agrippa, I was not disobedient unto the heavenly vision. . . . And as I thus spake for myself, Festus said with a loud voice, "Paul, thou art beside thyself; much learning doth make thee mad."

But I said, "I am not mad, most noble Festus; but speak forth the words of truth and soberness."

This episode obviously bears some resemblance to the encounter with the being of light in near death experiences. First of all, the being is endowed with personality, though no physical form is seen, and a "voice" which asks a question and issues instructions emanates from it. When Paul tries to tell others, he is mocked and labeled as "insane." Nonetheless, the vision changed the course of his life: He henceforth became the leading proponent of Christianity as a way of life entailing love of others.

There are differences, too, of course. Paul did not come near death in the course of his vision. Also, interestingly enough, Paul reports that he was blinded by the light and was unable to see for three days afterward. This runs contrary to the reports of those who say that though the light was indescribably brilliant, it in no way blinded them, or kept them from seeing things around them.

In his discussions of the nature of the afterlife, Paul says that some challenge the Christian concept of the afterlife by asking what kind of body the dead will have:

1 Corinthians 15:35-52: But some man will say, "How are the dead raised up? And with what body do they come?" Thou fool . . . (of) that which thou sowest, thou sowest not that body that shall be, but bare grain. . . . But God giveth it a body as it hath pleased him, and to every seed his own body. . . . There are also celestial bodies, and bodies terrestrial: but the glory of the celestial is one and the glory of the terrestrial is another. . . . So also is the resurrection of the dead. It is sown in corruption, it is raised in incorruption: It is sown in dishonor; it is raised in glory: It is sown in weakness; it is raised in power: It is sown a natural body, it is raised a spiritual body. There is a natural body, and there is a spiritual body. . . . Behold I show you a mystery: We shall not all sleep, but we shall all be changed. In a moment, in the twinkling of an eye, at the last trumpet: for the trumpet shall sound, and the dead shall be raised incorruptible.

Interestingly, Paul's brief sketch of the nature of the "spiritual body" corresponds very well with the accounts of those who have found themselves out of their bodies. In all cases, the immateriality of the spiritual body—its lack of physical substance—is stressed, as are its lack of limitations. Paul says, for example, that whereas the physical body was weak and ugly, the spiritual body will be strong and beautiful. This reminds one of the account of a near-death experience in which the spiritual body seemed whole and complete even when the physical body could be seen to be mutilated, and of another in which the spiritual body seemed to be of no particular age, *i.e.*, not limited by time.

Plato

The philosopher Plato, who was one of the greatest thinkers of all time, lived in Athens from 428 to 348 B.C. He left us a body of thought in the form of some twenty-two philosophical plays or dialogues, most of which include his teacher Socrates as chief interlocutor, and a small number of letters.

Plato believed strongly in the use of reason, logic, and argument in the attainment of truth and wisdom, but only up to a point, for in addition he was a great visionary who suggested that ultimately truth can only come to one in an almost mystical experience of enlightenment and insight. He accepted that there were planes and dimensions of reality other than the sensible, physical world and believed that the physical realm could be understood only by reference to these other, "higher" planes of reality. Accordingly, he was interested mainly in the incorporeal, conscious component of man—the soul—and saw the physical body only as the temporary vehicle of the soul. It is not surprising, then, that he was interested in the fate of the soul after physical death and that several of his dialogues—especially *Phaedo, Gorgias,* and *The Republic*—deal in part with that very topic.

Plato's writings are full of descriptions of death which are precisely like those which were discussed in the previous chapter. For instance, Plato defines death as the separation of the incorporeal part of a living person, the soul, from the physical part, the body. What is more, this incorporeal part of man is subject to many fewer limitations than is the physical part. Hence, Plato specifically points out that time is not an element of the realms beyond the physical, sensible world. The other realms are eternal, and, in Plato's striking phrase, what we call time is but the "moving, unreal reflection of eternity."

Plato discusses in various passages how the soul which has been separated from its body may meet and converse with the departed spirits of others and be guided through the transition from physical life to the next realm by guardian spirits. He mentions how some might expect to be met at the time of their death by a boat which takes them across a body of water to "the other shore" of their after-death existence. In *Phaedo* both the dramatic setting and the thrust of the arguments and words used drive home the point that the body is the prison of the soul and that, correspondingly, death is like an escape or release from that prison. While, as we saw in the first chapter, Plato articulates (through Socrates) the ancient view of death as a sleeping and a forgetting, he does so only ultimately to disavow it and, indeed, to turn it around 180°. According to Plato, the soul comes into the physical body from a higher and more divine realm of being. For him it is *birth* which is the sleeping and the forgetting, since the soul, in being born into the body, goes from a state of great awareness to a much less conscious one and in the meantime forgets the truths it knew while in its previous out-of-body state. Death, by implication, is an *awakening* and *remembering*. Plato remarks that the soul that has been separated from the body upon death can think and reason even more clearly than before, and that it can recognize things in their true nature far more readily. Furthermore, soon after death it faces a "judgment" in which a divine being displays before the soul all the things—both good and bad—which it has done in its life and makes the soul face them.

In Book X of *The Republic* perhaps the most striking similarity of all occurs. There Plato recounts the myth of Er, a Greek soldier. Er went away to a battle in which many Greeks were killed, and when his countrymen went to collect the bodies of their war dead his body was among them. It was lain, along with all the others, upon a funeral pyre to be burned. After some time his body revived, and Er described what he had seen in his journey to the realms beyond. First of all, Er said, his soul went out of his body, he joined with a group of other spirits, and they went to a place where there were "openings" or "passageways" apparently leading from earth into the realms of the afterlife. Here the other souls were stopped and judged by divine beings, who could see at a glance, in some sort of display, all the things that the soul had done while in its earthly life. Er, however, was not judged. Instead, the beings told him that he must go back to inform men in the physical world concerning what the other world was like. After seeing many other sights, Er was sent back, but he said that he was ignorant of how he was returned to his physical body. He merely woke up and found himself upon the funeral pyre.

It is important to bear in mind that Plato himself warns us that he meant his descriptions of the precise details of the world the soul will enter after death to be "probabilities, at best." Though he does not doubt that survival of bodily death does occur, he insists that in trying to explain the afterlife while still in our present physical life we face two strong disadvantages. First of all, our souls are imprisoned in physical bodies and are thus limited in what they can experience and learn by our physical senses. Vision, hearing, touch, taste, and smell each in its own way may fool us. Our eyes may make an enormous object seem small if it is far away, we may mishear what someone says to us, and so on. All this may result in our having false opinions or impressions of the nature of things. So, our souls cannot see reality in itself until they are liberated from the distractions and inaccuracies of the physical senses.

Secondly, Plato says human language is inadequate to express the ultimate realities directly. Words conceal rather than reveal the inner natures of things. It follows that no human words can do more than indicate—by analogy, through myth, and in other indirect ways—the true character of that which lies beyond the physical realm.

The Tibetan Book of the Dead

This remarkable work was compiled from the teachings of sages over many centuries in prehistoric Tibet and passed down through these early generations by word of mouth. It was finally written down, apparently, in the eighth century, A.D., but even then was hidden to keep it secret from outsiders.

The form which this unusual book takes is shaped by the many interrelated uses to which it was put. First of all, the wise men who wrote it regarded dying as, in effect, a skill—something which could be done either artfully or in an unbecoming manner, depending upon whether one had the requisite knowledge to do it well. So, the book was read as part of the funeral ceremony, or to the dying person during the closing moments of his life. It thus was thought to serve two functions. The first was to help the dying person keep in mind the nature of each new wondrous phenomenon as he experienced it. The second was to help those still living think positive thoughts and not hold the dying one back with their love and emotional concern, so that he could enter into the afterdeath planes in a proper frame of mind, released from all bodily concerns.

To effect these ends, the book contains a lengthy description of the various stages through which the soul goes after physical death. The correspondence between the early stages of death which it relates and those which have been recounted to me by those who have come near to death is nothing short of fantastic.

First of all, in the Tibetan account the mind or soul of the dying person departs from the body. At some time thereafter his soul enters a "swoon" and he finds himself in a void—not a physical void, but one which is, in effect, subject to its own kind of limits, and one in which his consciousness still exists. He may hear alarming and disturbing noises and sounds, described as roaring, thundering, and whistling noises, like the wind, and usually finds himself and his surroundings enveloped in a grey, misty illumination.

He is surprised to find himself out of his physical body. He sees and hears his relatives and friends mourning over his body and preparing it for the funeral and yet when he tries to respond to them they neither hear nor see him. He does not yet realize that he is dead, and he is confused. He asks himself whether he is dead or not, and, when he finally realizes that he is, wonders where he should go or what he should do. A great regret comes over him, and he is depressed about his state. For a while he remains near the places with which he has been familiar while in physical life.

He notices that he is still in a body—called the "shining" body—which does not appear to consist of material substance. Thus, he can go through rocks, walls, and even mountains without encountering any resistance. Travel is almost instantaneous. Wherever he wishes to be, he arrives there in only a moment. His thought and perception are less limited; his mind becomes very lucid and his senses seem more keen and more perfect and closer in nature to the divine. If he has been in physical life blind or deaf or crippled, he is surprised to find that in his "shining" body all his senses, as well as all the powers of his physical body, have been restored and intensified. He may encounter other beings in the same kind of body, and may meet what is called a clear or pure light. The Tibetans counsel the dying one approaching this light to try to have only love and compassion towards others.

The book also describes the feelings of immense peace and contentment which the dying one experiences, and also a kind of "mirror" in which his entire life, all deeds both good and bad, are reflected for both him and the beings judging him to see vividly. In this situation, there can be no misrepresentation; lying about one's life is impossible.

In short, even though *The Tibetan Book of the Dead* includes many later stages of death which none of my subjects have gone so far as to experience, it is quite obvious that there is a striking similarity between the account in this ancient manuscript and the events which have been related to me by twentieth-century Americans.

Emanuel Swedenborg

Swedenborg, who lived from 1688 untill 1772, was born in Stockholm, He was quite renowned in his day and made respectable contributions in various fields of natural science. His writings, at first oriented towards anatomy, physiology, and psychology, gained quite a bit of recognition. Later in his life, however, he underwent a religious crisis and began to tell of experiences in which he had purportedly been in communication with spiritual entities from beyond.

His later works abound with vivid descriptions of what life after death is like. Again, the correlation between what he writes of some of his spiritual experiences and what those who have come back from close calls with death report is amazing. For instance, Swedenborg describes how, when the bodily functions of respiration and circulation cease,

> Still man does not die, but is only separated from the corporeal part which was of use to him in the world. . . . Man, when he dies, only passes from one world into another.[2]

He claims that he himself has been through the early events of death, and has had experiences out of his body.

> I was brought into a state of insensibility as to the bodily senses, thus almost into the state of the dying; yet the interior life with thought remaining entire, so that I perceived and retained in memory the things which occurred, and which occur to those who are resuscitated from the dead. . . . Especially it was given to perceive . . . that there was a drawing and . . . pulling of . . . mind, thus of my spirit, from the body.

During this experience, he encounters beings whom he identifies as "angels." They ask him, in effect, if he is prepared to die.

> Those angels first inquired what my thought was, whether it was like the thought of those who die, which is usually about eternal life; and that they wished to keep my mind in that thought.

Yet, the communication which takes place between Swedenborg and the spirits is not of an earthly, human kind. It is instead almost a direct transfer of thoughts. Hence, there is no possibility of misunderstanding.

> Whereas spirits converse with each other by a universal language . . . Every man, immediately after death, comes into this universal language . . . which is proper to his spirit . . .
> The speech of an angel or a spirit with man is heard as sonorously as the speech of a man with a man; yet it is not heard by others who stand near, but by himself alone; the reason is, because the speech of an angel or spirit flows first into the man's thought . . .

The newly dead person does not realize that he is dead, for

he is still in a "body" which resembles his physical body in several respects.

> The first state of man after death is similar to his state in the world, because then in like manner he is in externals . . . Hence, he knows no otherwise than that he is still in the world. . . . Therefore, after they have wondered that they are in a body, and in every sense which they had in the world . . . they come into a desire of knowing what heaven is, and what hell is.

Yet, the spiritual state is less limited. Perception, thought, and memory are more perfect, and time and space no longer pose the obstacles they do in physical life.

> All the faculties of spirits . . . are in a more perfect state, their sensations as well as their thoughts and perceptions.

The dying man may meet with other departed spirits whom he knew while in life. They are there to help him during his passage into the beyond.

> The spirit of man recently departed from the world is . . . recognized by his friends, and by those whom he had known in the world . . . wherefore they are instructed by their friends concerning the state of eternal life. . . .

His past life may be shown to him in a vision. He remembers every detail of it, and there is no possibility of his lying or concealing anything.

> The interior memory . . . is such that there are inscribed in it all the particular things . . . which man has at any time thought, spoken, and done . . . from his earliest infancy to extreme old age. Man has with him the memory of all these things when he comes into another life, and is successively brought into all recollection of them. . . . All that he had spoken and done . . . are made manifest before the angels,

in a light as clear as day . . . and . . . there is nothing so concealed in the world that it is not manifested after death . . . as if seen in effigy, when the spirit is viewed in the light of heaven.

Swedenborg describes too the "light of the Lord" which permeates the hereafter, a light of ineffable brightness which he has glimpsed himself. It is a light of truth and of understanding.

So again in the writings of Swedenborg, as before in *The Bible*, the works of Plato, and *The Tibetan Book of the Dead*, we find striking parallels to the events of contemporary near-death experiences. The question naturally arises, though, as to whether this parallelism is really all that surprising. Some might suggest, for instance, that the authors of these various works could have influenced one another. Such an assertion could be supported in some cases, but not in others. Plato admits that he derived some of his insights partly from the religious mysticism of the East, so he might have been influenced by the same tradition which produced *The Tibetan Book of the Dead*. The ideas of Greek philosophy, in turn, influenced certain *New Testament* writers, and so it could be argued that Paul's discussion of the spiritual body has some of its roots in Plato.

On the other hand, in most cases it is not easy to establish that such influence could have taken place. Each writer seems to bring up a few interesting details which also recur in my interviews, yet which he could not have gotten from earlier authors. Swedenborg read *The Bible* and was familiar with Plato. However, he several times alludes to the fact that someone who has just died may not realize that he is dead for some time. This fact, which comes out again and again in the narratives of those who have come very close to death, is apparently not mentioned either in *The Bible* or by Plato. Yet, it is emphasized in *The Tibetan Book of the Dead*, a work which Swedenborg could not possibly have read. Indeed, it was not even translated until 1927.

Is it possible that the near-death experiences I have collected were influenced by works of the kind which I have discussed? All of the persons with whom I have talked had some exposure prior to their experiences to *The Bible*, and two or three knew something about the ideas of Plato. On the other hand, none were aware of the existence of such esoterica as the works of Swedenborg or *The Tibetan Book of the Dead*. Yet, many details which do not appear in *The Bible*, or even in Plato, constantly crop up in the accounts which I have gathered, and these correspond exactly with phenomena and events mentioned in the more unusual sources.

It must be acknowledged that the existence of the similarities and parallels among the writings of ancient thinkers and the reports of modern Americans who survive close brushes with death remains a striking, and, so far, not definitively explicable fact. How is it, we might well ask ourselves, that the wisdom of Tibetan sages, the theology and visions of Paul, the strange insights and myths of Plato, and the spiritual revelations of Swedenborg all agree so well, both among themselves and with the narratives of contemporary individuals who have come as close as anyone alive to the state of death?

[1]All quotations from *The Bible* are taken from the King James Version.

[2]All Swedenborg quotations are taken from *Compendium of the Theological and Spiritual Writings of Emanuel Swedenborg* (Boston: Crosby and Nichols, 1853), pp. 160-197.

IV.
QUESTIONS

By now, many doubts and objections will have occurred to the reader. In the years that I have been giving talks, in private and in public, on this subject, I have been asked many questions. In general, I tend to be asked about the same things on most occasions, so I have been able to compile a list of those questions which are asked most frequently. In this chapter and the next I shall address myself to them.

Are you just making all this up?

No, I'm not. I very much want to pursue a career in the teaching of psychiatry and the philosophy of medicine, and attempting to perpetrate a hoax would hardly be conducive to that aim.

Also, it has been my experience that anyone who makes

diligent and sympathetic inquiries among his own acquaintances, friends, and relatives about the occurrence of such experiences will soon have his doubts dispelled.

But aren't you being unrealistic? After all, how common are such experiences?

I am the first to admit that, due to the necessarily limited nature of my sample of cases, I am unable to give a statistically significant numerical estimate of the incidence or prevalence of this phenomenon. However, I am quite willing to say this: The occurrence of such experiences is far more common than anyone who hasn't studied them would guess. I have given many public lectures on this subject, to many kinds and sizes of groups, and there has never been an instance in which someone there didn't come up afterward with a story of his own, or even, in some cases, tell it publicly. Of course, one could always say (and truly!) that someone with such an experience would be more likely to come to a lecture on such a topic. Nonetheless, in many of the cases I have encountered, the person involved did not come to the lecture because of the topic. For example, I recently addressed a group of thirty persons. Two of them had had near-death experiences, and both were there just because they were members of the group. Neither knew the topic of my talk beforehand.

If near-death experiences are as common as you say, why isn't this fact more generally known?

There seem to be several reasons why this is so. First and foremost, I think, is the fact that the temper of our times is, in general, decidedly against discussion of the possibility of survival of bodily death. We live in an age in which science and technology have made enormous strides in understanding and conquering nature. To talk about life after death seems somehow atavistic to many who perhaps feel that the idea belongs more to our "superstitious" past than to our "scientific" present. Accordingly, persons who have experiences which lie outside the realm of science as we now understand it are ridiculed. Being aware of these attitudes, persons who have transcendent experiences are usually understandably reluctant to relate them very openly. I am convinced, in fact, that an enormous mass of material lies hidden in the minds of persons who have had such experiences but who, for fear of being labeled "crazy" or "over-imaginative," have never related them to more than one or two close friends or relatives.

In addition, the general public obscurity of the topic of near-death encounters seems to stem in part from a common psychological phenomenon involving attention. A lot of what we hear and see every day goes unregistered in our conscious minds. If our attention is drawn to something in a dramatic way, however, we tend to notice it thereafter. Many a person has had the experience of learning the meaning of a new word and then seeing the word in everything he picks up to read for the next few days. The explanation is usually not that the word has just taken hold in the language and is appearing everywhere. Rather, it is that the word has been there in the things he has been reading all along but that, not being aware of its meaning, he generally skipped over it without being consciously aware of it.

Similarly, after a lecture I recently gave I opened the floor for discussion and a doctor asking the first question said, "I have been in medicine for a long time. If these experiences are as commom as you say they are, why haven't I heard of them?" Knowing that there would probably be someone there who had encountered a case or two, I immediately turned the question back to the audience. I asked, "Has anyone else here heard of anything like this?" At this point, the doctor's wife raised her hand and related the story of a very close friend of theirs.

To give another example, a physician I know first became aware of experiences of this kind by reading an old newspaper article about a speech I gave. The next day, a patient gave him, unsolicited, an account of a very similar experience. The physician established that the patient could not have heard of or read about my studies. Indeed, the patient confided his story only because he was baffled and somewhat alarmed by what had happened to him and was seeking a medical opinion. It may very well have been that in both instances, the doctors involved had heard of some cases of this before, but had thought of them as individual quirks rather than as a wide-spread phenomenon and had not fully paid attention to them.

Finally, there is an additional factor in the case of physicians which may help to account for why so many of them seem unaware of near-death phenomena, even though one would suspect that doctors, of all people, should have encountered them. In the course of their training, it is constantly pounded into M.D.s-to-be that they must beware of what the patient says about the way he feels. A doctor is taught to pay close attention to the objective "signs" of disease processes, but to take the subjective reports ("symptoms") of the patient with a grain of salt. It is very reasonable to do it this way, because one can deal more readily with what is objective. However, this attitude also has the effect of hiding near-death experiences, since very few physicians make it a practice to ask about the feelings and perceptions of patients whom they resuscitate from clinical death. Because of this attitude, I would guess that doctors—who in theory should be the group most likely to uncover near-death experiences—are in fact not much more likely to hear of near-death experiences than are other persons.

Have you detected any differences between males and females with respect to this phenomenon?

There seems to be no difference at all in the contents or types of experiences reported by males and females. I have found both males and females who have described each of the common aspects of near-death encounters which have been discussed, and there is no one element which seems to weigh either more or less heavily in male vs. female reports.

Still, there are differences between male and female subjects. On the whole, males who have had near-death experiences are far more reticent to talk about them than are females. Far more males than females have told me briefly of experiences, only to fail to respond to my letters or return my calls when I tried to follow up with a more detailed interview. Many more males than females have made remarks such as "I tried to forget it, suppress it," often alluding to fears of ridicule, or intimating that the emotions involved in the experience were too overwhelming for them to recount.

Although I cannot offer any explanation of why this should be so, apparently I am not alone in noticing it. Dr. Russell Moores, a noted psychical researcher, has told me that he and others have observed the same thing. About one-third as many men as women come to him reporting a psychical experience.

Another interesting fact is that a somewhat larger number of these experiences than would be expected took place during pregnancy. Again, I can't explain why this should be. Perhaps it is only that pregnancy is in itself a rather risky physiological state in many ways, attendant with many potential medical complications. Coupled with the fact that only women get pregnant, and that women are less reticent than men to talk, this might help explain the frequency of experiences taking place during pregnancy.

How do you know that all these people aren't just lying to you?

It is quite easy for persons who have not listened and watched as others have related near-death experiences intellectually to entertain the hypothesis that these stories are lies. However, I find myself in a rather unique position. I have witnessed mature, emotionally stable adults—both men and women—break down and weep while telling me of events that happened up to three decades before. I have detected in their voices sincerity, warmth, and feeling which cannot really be conveyed in a written recounting. So to me, in a way that is unfortunately impossible for many others to share, the notion that these accounts might be fabrications is utterly untenable.

In addition to the weight of my own opinion, there are some strong considerations which should rule heavily against the fabrication hypothesis. The most obvious is the difficulty of explaining the similarity of so many of the accounts. How is it that many people just happen to have come up with the same lie to tell me over a period of eight years? Collusion remains a theoretical possibility here. It is certainly conceivable that a nice elderly lady from eastern North Carolina, a medical student from New Jersey, a Georgia veterinarian, and many others several years ago banded together and conspired to carry out an elaborate hoax against me. However, I don't regard this to be a very likely possibility!

If they are not overtly lying, perhaps they are misrepresenting in a more subtle way. Isn't it possible that over the years, they have elaborated their stories?

This question points to the well-known psychological phenomenon in which a person may start with a fairly simple account of an experience or event and over a period of time develop it into a very elaborate narrative. With each telling, a subtle detail is added, the speaker coming eventually to believe it himself, until at last the story is so embellished as to bear little resemblance to the original.

I do not believe that this mechanism has been operative to any significant degree in the cases I have studied, however. In the first place, the accounts of persons whom I have interviewed very soon after their experience—in some cases, while they were still in the hospital recovering—are of the same type as those of people who have recounted experiences which took place decades ago. Further, in a few cases, persons whom I have interviewed wrote down descriptions of their experiences shortly after they happened and read to me from their notes during the interview. Again, these descriptions are of the same sort as experiences which are recounted from memory after lapses of some years. Also, there is the fact that quite often I have been only the first or second person to whom an experience has been related, and then only with great reluctance, even in cases where the experience happened some years before. Though there has been little or no opportunity for embellishment in such cases, these accounts, again, are no different as a group from those accounts that have been retold more often over a period of years. Finally, it is quite possible that in many cases, the reverse of embellishment has taken place. What psychiatrists call "suppression" is a mental mechanism whereby a conscious effort is made to control undesired memories, feelings, or thoughts or to conceal them from awareness. On numerous occasions in the course of interviews, persons have made remarks which are strongly indicative that suppression has occurred. For example, one woman who reported to me a very elaborate experience which took place during her "death" said, "I feel that there is more to it, but I can't remember it all. I tried to suppress it because I knew people weren't going to believe me anyway." A man who suffered a cardiac arrest during surgery for major wounds received in Viet Nam related his difficulty in dealing with his out-of-body experiences emotionally. "I get choked up by trying to tell about it even now. . . . I feel that there is a lot I don't remember about it. I have tried to forget it." In short, it seems that a strong case can be made that embellishment has not been a very significant factor in the development of these stories.

Did all these people profess a religion before their experiences?
If so, aren't the experiences shaped by their religious beliefs
and backgrounds?

They seem to be to some extent. As mentioned earlier, though the description of the being of light is invariable, the identity ascribed to it varies, apparently as a function of the religious background of the individual. Through all of my research, however, I have not heard a single reference to a heaven or a hell anything like the customary picture to which we are exposed in this society. Indeed, many persons have stressed how unlike their experiences were to what they had been led to expect in the course of their religious training. One woman who "died" reported: "I had always heard that when you die, you see both heaven and hell, but I didn't see either one." Another lady who had an out-of-body experience after severe injuries said, "The strange thing was that I had always been taught in my religious upbringing that the minute you died you would be right at these beautiful gates, pearly gates. But there

I was hovering around my own physical body, and that was it! I was just baffled." Furthermore, in quite a few instances reports have come from persons who had no religious beliefs or training at all prior to their experiences, and their descriptions do not seem to differ in content from people who had quite strong religious beliefs. In a few cases, someone who had been exposed to religious doctrines but had rejected them earlier in life acquired religious feelings with new depth after the experience. Others say that although they had read religious writings, such as *The Bible*, they had never really understood certain things they had read there until their near-death experiences.

What bearing, if any, do the experiences which you have studied have on the possibility of reincarnation?

Not one of the cases I have looked into is in any way indicative to me that reincarnation occurs. However, it is important to bear in mind that not one of them rules out reincarnation, either. If reincarnation does occur, it seems likely that an interlude in some other realm would occur between the time of separation from the old body and the entry into the new one. Accordingly, the technique of interviewing people who came back from close calls with death would not be the proper mode for studying reincarnation, anyway.

Other methods can and have been tried in investigating reincarnation. For example, some have tried the technique of "far age regression." A subject is hypnotized and the suggestion is made to him that he go back mentally to successively earlier and earlier times in his life. When he reaches the time of the earliest experiences he can recall in his present life, he is then told to try to go back even beyond that! At this point, many persons begin telling elaborate stories about previous lives in earlier times and distant places. In some cases, such stories check out with remarkable accuracy. This has happened even when it can be established that the subject could not have known in any normal way about the events, persons, and places he describes so accurately. The case of Bridey Murphy is the most famous, but there are many others, some even more impressive and well-documented, which are not as widely known. Readers who wish to pursue this question further are referred to the excellent study, *Twenty Cases Suggestive of Reincarnation*, by Ian Stevenson, M.D. It is also worth noting that *The Tibetan Book of the Dead*, which so accurately recounts the stages of near-death encounters, says that reincarnation does occur at some later point, after the events which have been related by my subjects.

Have you ever interviewed anyone who has had a near-death experience in association with a suicide attempt? If so, was the experience any different?

I do know of a few cases in which a suicide attempt was the cause of the apparent "death." These experiences were uniformly characterized as being unpleasant.

As one woman said, "If you leave here a tormented soul, you will be a tormented soul over there, too." In short, they report that the conflicts they had attempted suicide to escape were still present when they died, but with added complications. In their disembodied state they were unable to do anything about their problems, and they also had to view the unfortunate consequences which resulted from their acts.

A man who was despondent about the death of his wife shot himself, "died" as a result, and was resuscitated. He states:

I didn't go where [my wife] was. I went to an awful place. . . . I immediately saw the mistake I had made. . . . I thought, "I wish I hadn't done it."

Others who experienced this unpleasant "limbo" state have remarked that they had the feeling they would be there for a long time. This was their penalty for "breaking the rules" by trying to release themselves prematurely from what was, in effect, an "assignment"—to fulfill a certain purpose in life.

Such remarks coincide with what has been reported to me by several people who "died" of other causes but who said that, while they were in this state, it had been intimated to them that suicide was a very unfortunate act which attended with a severe penalty. One man who had a near-death experience after an accident said:

> [While I was over there] I got the feeling that two things it was completely forbidden for me to do would be to kill myself or to kill another person. . . . If I were to commit suicide, I would be throwing God's gift back in his face. . . . Killing somebody else would be interfering with God's purpose for that individual.

Sentiments like these, which by now have been expressed to me in many separate accounts, are identical to those embodied in the most ancient theological and moral argument against suicide—one which occurs in various forms in the writings of thinkers as diverse as St. Thomas Aquinas, Locke, and Kant. A suicide, in Kant's view, is acting in opposition to the purposes of God and arrives on the other side viewed as a rebel against his creator. Aquinas argues that life is a gift from God and that it is God's prerogative, not man's, to take it back.

In discussing this, however, I do not pass a moral judgment against suicide. I only report what others who have been through this experience have told me. I am now in the process of preparing a second book on near-death experiences, in which this topic, along with others, will be dealt with at greater length.

Do you have any cross-cultural cases?

No, I don't. In fact, one of the many reasons I say that my study is not "scientific" is that the group of individuals to whom I have listened is not a random sample of human beings. I would be very interested in hearing about the near-death experiences of Eskimos, Kwakiutl Indians, Navahos, Watusi tribesmen, and so on. However, due to geographic and other limitations, I have not been able to locate any.

Are there any historical examples of near-death phenomena?

As far as I know, there are not. However, since I have been fully occupied with contemporary instances, I have simply not had the time adequately to research this question. So I would not at all be surprised to find that such reports have been recounted in the past. On the other hand, I strongly suspect that near-death experiences have been vastly more common in the past few decades than in earlier periods. The reason for this is simply that it has only been in fairly recent times that advanced resuscitation technology has been available. Many of the people who have been brought back in our era would not have survived in earlier years. Injections of adrenalin into the heart, a machine which delivers a shock to the heart, and artificial heart and lung machines are examples of such medical advances.

Have you investigated the medical records of your subjects?

In so far as possible, I have. In the cases I have been invited to investigate, the records have borne out the assertions of the persons involved. In some cases, due to the passage of time and/or the death of the persons who carried out the resuscitation, records are not available. The reports for which substantiating records are not available are no different from those in which records are available. In many instances when medical records have not been accessible, I have secured the testimony of others— friends, doctors, or relatives of the informant—to the effect that the near-death event did occur.

I have heard that, after five minutes, resuscitation is impossible, yet you say that some of your cases have been "dead" for up to twenty minutes. How is this possible?

Most numbers and quantities one hears quoted in medical practice are means, averages, and are not to be taken as absolutes. The figure of five minutes which one often hears quoted is an average. It is a clinical rule of thumb not to attempt resuscitation after five minutes because, in most instances, brain damage from lack of oxygen would have occurred beyond that time. However, since it is only an average, one would expect individual cases to fall on either side of it. I have in fact found cases in which resuscitation took place after twenty minutes with no evidence of brain damage.

Were any of these people really dead?

One of the main reasons why this question is so confusing and difficult to answer is that it is partly a semantic question involving the meaning of the word "dead." As the recent heated controversy surrounding the transplantation of organs reveals, the definition of "death" is by no means settled, even among professionals in the field of medicine. Criteria of death vary not only between laymen and physicians, but also among physicians and from hospital to hospital. So, the answer to this question will depend on what is meant by "dead." It will be profitable here to look at three definitions in turn and to comment upon them.

1. "DEATH" AS THE ABSENCE OF CLINICALLY DETECTABLE VITAL SIGNS.

Some will be willing to say that a person is "dead" if his heart stops beating and he quits breathing for an extended period of time, his blood pressure drops as low as to be unreadable, his pupils dilate, his body temperature begins to go down, etc. This is the clinical definition, and it has been employed for centuries by physicians and laymen alike. In fact, most people who have ever been pronounced dead were adjudged so on the basis of this criterion.

There is no question but that this clinical standard was met in many of the cases I have studied. Both the testimony of physicians and the evidence of medical records adequately support the contention that "deaths" in this sense did take place.

2. "DEATH" AS THE ABSENCE OF BRAIN WAVE ACTIVITY.

The advancement of technology has brought the development of more sensitive techniques for detecting biological processes, even those which might not be observable overtly. The electroencephalograph (EEG) is a machine which amplifies and records the minute electrical potentials of the brain. Recently, the trend has been to base assessment of "real" death on the absence of electrical activity in the brain, as determined by the presence of "flat" EEG tracings.

Obviously, in all of the cases of resuscitation which I have dealt with, there was an extreme clinical emergency. There was no time to set up an EEG; the clinicians were rightly concerned about doing what they could to get their patient back. So, some might argue that none of these persons can be adjudged to have been "dead."

Suppose for a moment, however, that "flat" EEG readings had been obtained on a large percentage of the persons who were thought dead and were then resuscitated. Would that fact necessarily add very much here? I think not, for three reasons. First, resuscitation attempts are always emergencies, which last at the very most for thirty minutes or so. Setting up an EEG machine is a very complicated and technical task, and it is fairly common for even an experienced technician to have to work with it for some time to get correct readings, even under optimum conditions. In an emergency, with its accompanying confusion, there would probably be an increased likelihood of mistakes. So, even if one could present a flat EEG tracing for a person who told of a near-death experience, it would still be possible for a critic to say—with justice—that the tracing might not be accurate.

Second, even the marvelous electric brain machine, properly set up, does not enable us infallibly to determine whether resuscitation is possible in any given case. Flat EEG tracings have been obtained in persons who were later resuscitated. Overdoses of drugs which are depressants of the central nervous system, as well as hypothermia (low body temperature) have both resulted in this phenomenon.

Third, even if I could produce a case in which it could be established that the machine was correctly set up, there would still be a problem. Someone could say that there is no proof that the reported near-death experience took place during the time the EEG was flat, but rather before or afterwards. I conclude, then, that the EEG is not very valuable at this present stage of investigation.

3. "DEATH" AS AN IRREVERSIBLE LOSS OF VITAL FUNCTIONS.

Others will adopt an even more restricted definition, holding that one cannot say that a person was ever "dead," no matter how long his vital signs were clinically undetectable, and no matter how long his EEG was flat, if he was subsequently resuscitated. In other words, "death" is defined as that state of the body from which it is impossible to be revived. Obviously, by this definition, none of my cases would qualify, since they all involved resuscitation.

We have seen, then, that the answer to the question depends upon what is meant by "dead." One must remember that even though this is in part a semantic dispute, it is nonetheless an important issue, because all three definitions embody important insights. In fact, I would agree with the third, most stringent definition to some extent. Even in those cases in which the heart was not beating for extended periods, the tissues of the body, particularly the brain, must somehow have been perfused (supplied with oxygen and nourishment) most of the time. It is not necessary that one assume in any of these cases that any law of biology or physiology was violated. In order for resuscitation to have occurred, some degree of residual biological activity must have been going on in the cells of the body, even though the overt signs of these processes were not clinically detectable by the methods employed. However, it seems that it is impossible at present to determine exactly what the point of no return is. It may well vary with the individual, and it is likely not a fixed point but rather a shifting range on a continuum. In fact, a few decades ago most of the people with whom I have talked could not have been brought back. In the future, techniques might become available which would enable us to revive people who can't be saved today.

Let us, therefore, hypothesize that death is a separation of the mind from the body, and that the mind does pass into other realms of existence at this point. It would follow that there exists some mechanism whereby the soul or mind is released upon death. One has no basis upon which to assume, though, that this mechanism works exactly in accordance with what we have in our own era somewhat arbitrarily taken to be the point of no return. Nor do we have to assume that it works perfectly in every instance, any more than we have to assume that any bodily system always works perfectly. Perhaps this mechanism might sometime come into play even before any physiological crisis, affording a few persons a brief glimpse of other realities. This would help to account for the reports of those persons who have had flashbacks of their lives, out-of-body experiences, etc., when they felt certain that they were about to be killed, even before any physical injury occured.

All I ultimately want to claim is this: Whatever that point of irretrievable death is said to be—whether in the past, present, or future—those with whom I have talked have been much closer to it than have the vast majority of their fellow human beings. For this reason alone, I am quite willing to listen to what they have to say.

In the final analysis, though, it is quite pointless to cavil over the precise definition of "death"—irreversible or otherwise— in the context of this discussion. What the person who raises such objections to near-death experiences seems to have in mind is something more basic. He reasons that as long as it remains a possibility that there was some residual biological activity in the body, then that activity might have caused, and thus account for, the experience.

Now, I granted earlier that there must have been some residual biological function in the body in all cases. So, the issue of whether a "real" death occurred really reduces to the more basic problem of whether the residual biological function could account for the occurrence of the experiences. In other words:

Aren't other explanations (i.e., other than survival of bodily death) possible?

This in turn brings us to the topic of the next chapter.

V.
EXPLANATIONS

Of course alternative "explanations" of near-death phenomena are available. In fact, from the purely philosophical point of view, an infinity of hypotheses could be constructed to explain any experience, observation, or fact. That is, one could go on forever manufacturing more and more theoretically possible explanations for anything one wanted to explain. It is the same in the case of near-death experiences; all sorts of possible explanations present themselves.

Out of the many kinds of explanations which might theoretically be proposed, there are a few which have been suggested quite frequently in the audiences which I have addressed. Accordingly, I shall now deal with these more common explanations, and with another which, though it has never been proposed to me, might well have been. I have somewhat arbitrarily divided them into three types: Supernatural, Natural (Scientific), and Psychological.

Supernatural Explanations

Rarely, someone in one of my audiences has proposed demonic explanations of near-death experiences, suggesting that the experiences were doubtless directed by inimical forces. As a response to such explanations, I can only say this. It seems to me that the best way of distinguishing between God-directed and Satan-directed experiences would be to see what the person involved does and says after his experience. God, I suppose, would try to get those to whom he appears to be loving and forgiving. Satan would presumably tell his servants to follow a course of hate and destruction. Manifestly, my subjects have come back with a renewed commitment to follow the former course and to disavow the latter. In the light of all the machinations which a hypothetical demon would have to have carried out in order to delude his hapless victim (and to what purpose?), he certainly has failed miserably—as far as I can tell—to make persuasive emissaries for his program!

Natural (Scientific) Explanations

1. THE PHARMACOLOGICAL EXPLANATION

Some suggest that near-death experiences are caused by the therapeutic drugs administered to the person at the time of his crisis. The surface plausibility of this view derives from several facts. For example, it is generally agreed by most medical scientists and laymen that certain drugs cause delusional and hallucinatory mental states and experiences. Furthermore, we are now passing through an era in which there is intense interest in the problem of drug abuse, and much public attention has focused on the illicit use of drugs such as LSD, marijuana, and so forth, which do appear to cause such hallucinatory episodes. Finally, there is the fact that even many medically-accepted drugs are associated with various effects on the mind which may resemble the events of the experience of dying. For example, the drug ketamine (or cyclohexanone) is an intravenously injected anesthetic with side effects which are similar in some respects to out-of-body experiences. It is classified as a "dissociative" anesthetic because during induction the patient may become unresponsive not only to pain but also to the environment as a whole. He feels "dissociated" from his environment, including the parts of his own body—his legs, arms, and so forth. For a time after recovery, he may be left with psychological disturbances, including hallucinations and very vivid dreams. (Note that a few persons have used this very word—"dissociation"—to characterize their feelings while in the out-of-body state.)

What is more, I have collected a few accounts from people who, while under anesthetics, had what they plainly identified as hallucinatory-type visions of death. Let me give one example.

It was some time in my early teen-age years, I was in the dentist's office for a filling and was given nitrous oxide. I was kind of nervous about taking it, because I was afraid I wouldn't wake up again. As the anesthesia began to take effect, I felt myself going around in a spiral. It wasn't like I was turning around, but like the dentist's chair was moving in a spiral upward, and it was going up and up and up.

Everything was very bright and white and as I got to the top of the spiral, angels came down to meet me and to take me to heaven. I use the plural, "angels," because it's very vague but I'm sure that there were more than one. Yet I can't say how many.

At one point the dentist and nurse were talking to each other about another person, and I heard them, but by the time they finished a sentence I couldn't even remember what the first of the sentence had been. But I knew they were talking, and as they did their words would echo around and around. It was an echo that seemed to get

further and further away, like in the mountains. I do remember that I seemed to hear them from above, because I
felt as though I was up high, going to heaven.

That's all I remember except that I hadn't been afraid or
panicked at the thought of dying. At that time in my life, I
was afraid of going to hell, but when this happened there
was no question in my mind but that I was going to heaven.
I was very surprised later that the thought of death hadn't
bothered me, but finally it dawned on me that in my
anesthetized state nothing bothered me. The whole thing
was just happy because I'm sure the gas made me completely carefree. I blamed it on that. It was such a vague
thing. I didn't dwell on it afterwards.

Notice that there are a few points of similarity between this
experience and some others which have been taken to be real
by those to whom they happened. This woman describes a
brilliant white light, meeting others who are there to take her
to the other side, and lack of concern over being dead. There
are also two aspects which suggest an out-of-body experience:
Her impression that she heard the voices of the dentist and
nurse from a position above them, and her feeling of "floating."

On the other hand, other details of this story are very atypi-
cal of near-death experiences which are reported as having
actually happened. The brilliant light is not personified and no
ineffable feelings of peace and happiness occurred. The description of the after-death world is very literalistic and, she
says, in accordance with her religious training. The beings who
met her are identified as "angels," and she talks of going to a
"heaven" which is located in the "up" direction, where she is
headed. She denies seeing her body or being in any other kind
of body, and she plainly feels that the dentist's chair, and not her
own motion, was the source of the rotatory movement. She
repeatedly stresses the vagueness of her experience, and it
apparently had no effect on her belief in an afterlife. (In fact,
she now has doubts about survival of bodily death.)

In comparing reports in which the experience is plainly
attributed to a drug with near-death experiences which are

reported as real, several points need to be mentioned. First of all, the few people who have described such "drug" experiences to me are no more and no less romantic, imaginative, intelligent, or stable than are the persons reporting "real" near-death experiences. Secondly, these drug-induced experiences are extremely vague. Thirdly, the stories vary among themselves, and also markedly from the "real" near-death visions. I should say that in choosing the specific case of the "anesthetic" type of experience to be used, I have purposefully chosen the one which *most closely resembles* the group of "real" experiences. So, I would suggest that there are, in general, very great differences between these two types of experiences.

Furthermore, there are many additional factors which rule against the pharmacological explanation of near-death phenomena. The most significant one is simply that in many cases no drug had been administered prior to the experience nor, in some cases, were drugs given even after the near-death event. In fact, many persons have made it a point to insist to me that the experience clearly took place before any kind of medication was given, in some cases long before they obtained any sort of medical attention. Even in those instances in which therapeutic drugs were administered around the time of the near-death event, the variety of drugs employed for different patients is enormous. They range from substances such as aspirin through antibiotics and the hormone adrenalin to local and gaseous anesthetics. Most of these drugs are not associated with central nervous system or psychic effects. It also should be noted that there are no differences as groups between the experiences related by those who were given no drugs at all and the experiences related by those who were under medications of various types. Finally, I shall note without comment that one woman who "died" twice on separate occasions some years apart attributed her *lack* of an experience the first time to her anesthetized condition. The second time, when she was under no drugs at all, she had a very complex experience.

One of the assumptions of modern medical pharmacology is the notion, which also seems to have gained acceptance among the great mass of laymen in our society, that psychoactive drugs *cause* the psychic episodes with which their use is associated. These psychic events are therefore considered to be "unreal," "hallucinatory," "delusional," or "only in the mind." One must remember, however, that this view is by no means universally accepted; there is another view of the relationship between drugs and experiences attending their use. I refer to the initiatory and exploratory use of what we call "hallucinogenic"drugs. Through the ages men have turned to such psychoactive compounds in their quest to achieve other states of consciousness and to reach other planes of reality. (For a lively and fascinating contemporary exposition of this side of drug use, see the recent book, *The Natural Mind*, by Andrew Weil, M.D.) Thus, drug use has historically been associated, not only with medicine and the treatment of disease, but also with religion and the attainment of enlightenment. For example, in the well-publicized rituals of the peyote cult found among American Indians in the western United States, the peyote cactus plant (which contains the substance mescaline) is ingested in order to attain religious visions and enlightenment. There are similar cults all over the world, and their members share the belief that the drug they employ provides a means of passage into other dimensions of reality. Assuming this viewpoint to be valid, it could be hypothesized that drug use would be only one pathway among many leading to the achievement of enlightenment and to the discovery of other realms of existence. The experience of dying could, then, be another such pathway, and all this would help to account for the resemblance of drug-induced experiences like the one given above to near-death experiences.

2. PHYSIOLOGICAL EXPLANATIONS

Physiology is that branch of biology which deals with the functions of the cells, organs and whole bodies of living beings, and with the interrelationships among these functions. A physiological explanation of near-death phenomena which I have often heard proposed is that, since the oxygen supply to the brain is cut off during clinical death and some other kinds of severe bodily stress, the phenomena perceived must represent some sort of last compensatory gasp of the dying brain.

The main thing wrong with this hypothesis is simply this: As can easily be seen from a survey of the dying experiences reported earlier, many of the near-death experiences happened before any physiological stress of the required type took place. Indeed, in a few cases there was no bodily injury at all during the encounter. Yet, every single element which appears in cases of severe injury can also be seen in other instances in which injury was not involved.

3. NEUROLOGICAL EXPLANATIONS

Neurology is the medical specialty dealing with the cause, diagnosis, and treatment of diseases of the nervous system (that is the brain, spinal cord, and nerves). Phenomena similar to those reported by persons who nearly die show up also in certain neurological conditions. So, some might propose neurological explanations of near-death experiences in terms of supposed malfunctions in the nervous system of the dying person. Let us consider neurological parallels for two of the more striking events of the dying experience: The instantaneous "review" of the events of the dying person's life and the out-of-body phenomenon.

I encountered a patient on the neurology ward at a hospital who described a peculiar form of seizure disorder in which he saw flashbacks of events in his earlier life.

The first time it happened, I was looking at a friend of mine across the room. The right side of his face just kind of became distorted. All of a sudden, there was an intrusion into my consciousness of scenes of things that had happened in the past. They were just like they were when they actually happened—vivid, completely in color, and three-dimensional. I felt nauseated, and I was so startled that I tried to avoid the images. Since then, I've had many of these attacks, and I've learned just to let it run its course. The closest parallel I can draw to it is the films they have on television at New Year's. Scenes of things that happened that year are flashed on the screen and when you see one, it's gone before you can really think about it. That's how it is with these attacks. I'll see something and think, "Oh, I remember that." And I'll try to keep it in my mind, but another is flashed up before I can.

The images are things that really happened. Nothing is modified. When it is over, though, it is very difficult to recall what images I saw. Sometimes, it's the same images, other times not. As they appear I remember, "Oh, these are the same ones I've seen before," but when it's over it's almost impossible to recall what they were. They don't seem to be particularly significant events in my life. In fact, none of them are. They all seem very trivial. They don't happen in any sort of order, not even in the order they happened in my life. They just come at random.

When the images come, I can still see what's going on around me, but my awareness is diminished. I'm not as sharp. It's almost as if half of my mind is taken up with the images, and the other half is on what I'm doing. People who have seen me during an attack say that it just lasts about a minute, but to me it seems like ages.

There are certain obvious similarities between these seizures, which doubtless were occasioned by a focus of irritation in the brain, and the panoramic memory reported by some of my near-death subjects. For example, this man's seizure took the form of visual images which were incredibly vivid and were actually three-dimensional. Further, the images just seemed to come to him, quite apart from any intention on his part. He also reports that the images came with great rapidity and he emphasizes the distortion of his senses of time which went along with the seizure.

On the other hand, there are striking differences as well. Unlike those seen in near-death experiences, the memory images did not come in the order of his life, nor were they seen all at once, in a unifying vision. They were not highlights or significant events in his life; he stresses their triviality. Thus, they did not seem to be presented to him for judgmental or educational purposes. While many near-death subjects point out that after their "review" they could remember the events of their life with much greater clarity and in more detail than before, this man states that he could not remember what the particular images were following the seizure.

Out-of-body experiences have a neurological analogue in so-called "autoscopic (self-seeing) hallucinations," which are the subject of an excellent article by Dr. N. Lukianowicz in the medical journal, *Archives of Neurology and Psychiatry*. In these odd visions, the subject sees a projection of himself into his own visual field. This strange "double" mimics the facial expressions and other bodily movements of its original, who is completely baffled and confused when he suddenly sees an image of himself at a distance from himself, usually straight ahead.

Though this experience is clearly somewhat analogous to the out-of-body visions described earlier, the differences heavily outweigh the similarities. The autoscopic phantom is always perceived as alive—sometimes it is thought of by the subject as even more alive and conscious than he is—while in out-of-body experiences the body is seen as something lifeless, just a shell. The autoscopic subject may "hear" his double talk to him, give him instructions, taunt him, and so on. While in out-of-body experiences the whole body is seen (unless it is partly covered up or otherwise concealed), the autoscopic double is far more frequently seen only from the chest or neck up.

In fact, autoscopic copies have many more features in common with what I have called the spiritual body than with the physical body which is seen by a dying person. Autoscopic doubles, though sometimes seen in color, are more often described as wispy, transparent, and colorless. The subject may in fact see his image walk through doors or or other physical obstacles without any apparent trouble.

I present here an account of an apparent autoscopic hallucination which was described to me. It is unique in that it involved two persons simultaneously.

About eleven o'clock one summer night about two years before my wife and I were married, I was driving her home in my sports convertible. I parked the car on the dimly-lit street in front of her house, and we were both surprised as we both looked up at the same time and saw huge images of ourselves, from the waist up and sitting side by side, in the big trees which hung over the street about one hundred feet directly ahead of us. The images were dark, almost like silhouettes, and we couldn't see through them at all, but they were quite exact replicas, anyway. Neither of us had any trouble recognizing both of them at once. They moved around, but not in imitation of our movements, since we were just sitting still watching them. They did things such as: My image picked up a book and showed something in it to the image of my wife, and she leaned over and looked more closely at the book.

As we sat there, I would narrate the scene for a while—tell my wife what I saw the images doing—and what I said was exactly what she had been seeing them doing. Then we would switch. She would tell me what she was seeing them doing, and it would be exactly what I had seen.

We sat there for a long time—at least thirty minutes—watching this and talking about it as we watched it. I guess we could have gone on like that for the rest of the night. My wife had to go in, though, so we finally just walked together up the steps going up the hill to her house. When I came back down, I saw the images again, and they were still there as I drove away.

There is no chance that this was any sort of reflection of us in the windshield because the top of the car was down and we were looking way up over the windshield to see them the whole time. Neither of us ever drank, either—and we still don't—and this was three years before we had even heard anything about LSD or drugs like that. We weren't tired, either, even though it was fairly late, so we weren't asleep and dreaming it. We were very awake, alert, amazed, and excited as we watched the images and talked about them with each other.

Granted, autoscopic hallucinations are in some ways like the out-of-body phenomenon associated with a near-death experience. However, even if we were to focus on all the points of similarity and to neglect the differences entirely, the existence of autoscopic hallucinations would not give us an explanation for the occurrence of out-of-body experiences. The simple reason is that there is no explanation for autoscopic hallucinations, either. Many conflicting explanations have been proposed by different neurologists and psychiatrists, but they are still debated, and no one theory has gained general acceptance. So, to try to explain all out-of-body experiences as autoscopic hallucinations would only be to substitute a bafflement for an enigma.

Finally, there is another point which is relevant to the discussion of neurological explanations for near-death experiences. In one case I found a subject who had a residual neurological problem deriving from a near-death encounter. The problem was a very mild deficit consisting of the partial paralysis of a small group of muscles on one side of the body. Though I have often asked whether there were any residual deficits, this is the only example I have found of neurological damage following a near-death encounter.

Psychological Explanations

Psychology has not yet attained anything approaching the degree of rigor and precision which some other sciences have reached in the modern age. Psychologists are still divided into contesting schools of thought with conflicting viewpoints, investigative approaches, and fundamental understandings about the existence and nature of the mind. Psychological explanations of near-death experiences, therefore, will vary widely according to the school of thought to which the explainer belongs. Instead of considering each type of psychological explanation which might possibly be proposed, I shall stick to a few which I have heard most often from members of my audience, and to one which has struck me as in a way the most tempting.

I touched earlier on two commonly proposed psychological type explanations—those which hypothesize that either conscious lying or unconscious embellishment might have occurred. In the present chapter I want to consider two others.

1. ISOLATION RESEARCH

In all of the public lectures I have presented on my studies, no one has ever advanced an explanation of near-death experiences in terms of the results of isolation research. Yet it is in precisely this relatively recent and rapidly growing area of behavioral science that phenomena most closely resembling the stages of the experience of dying have been studied and produced under laboratory conditions.

Isolation research is the study of what happens to the mind and body of a person who is isolated in one way or another; for example, by being removed from all social contact with other humans, or by being subjected to a monotonous, repetitive task for long periods.

Data on situations of this type has been gathered in several ways. Written accounts of the experiences of lone polar explorers or of solitary survivors of shipwrecks contain much information. During the last few decades, researchers have attempted to investigate similar phenomena under laboratory conditions. One well-publicized technique has been to suspend a volunteer in a tank of water which is the same temperature as his body. This minimizes sensations of weight and temperature. He is blindfolded and his ears are fitted with plugs to intensify the effect of the dark, sound-proofed tank. His arms are constrained in tubes so that he cannot move them, and he is thus deprived of many of the normal sensations of joint movement and position.

Under these and other solitary conditions, some people have

experienced unusual psychological phenomena, many of which strongly resemble those I outlined in Chapter 2. One woman who spent long periods alone in the desolate conditions of the North Pole reports a panoramic vision of the events of her life. Shipwrecked sailors stranded alone in small boats for many weeks have described hallucinations of being rescued, sometimes by paranormal beings almost like ghosts or spirits. This bears vague analogies to the being of light or departed spirits whom many of my subjects have encountered. Other near-death type phenomena which recur in accounts of isolation experiences include: Distortions of sense of time, feelings of being partly dissociated from the body, resistance to going back to civilization or leaving isolation, and feelings of being "at one" with the universe. In addition, many who have been isolated by shipwreck or other such events say that after a few weeks of being in this condition, they came back to civilization with a profound change of values. They may report that afterwards they feel inwardly more secure. Clearly, this reintegration of personality is similar to that claimed by many who have come back from death.

Likewise, there are certain aspects of dying situations that are much like the features found in isolation experiences and studies. Patients who come near death are often isolated and immobile in the recovery rooms of hospitals, often in conditions of subdued sound and light and with no visitors. One might even wonder whether the physiological changes associated with the death of the body could produce a radical kind of isolation resulting in an almost total cut-off of sensory input to the brain. Further, as was discussed at length earlier, many near-death patients have told me of the distressing feelings of isolation, of loneliness, and of being cut off from human contact which came over them when they were out of their bodies.

Indeed, one could no doubt find borderline cases which could not be classified clearly either as near-death experiences or as isolation experiences. For example, one man gave me the following story of his stay in the hospital during a severe illness.

I was extremely ill in the hospital, and as I lay there I

kept seeing pictures coming at me, just as though they were on a television screen. The pictures were of people, and I could see a person, as though out in space at a distance, and it would start coming toward me, then it would go past and another one would appear. I was perfectly aware that I was in the hospital room and was sick, but I started to wonder what was going on. Now, some of these people I knew personally—they were friends and relatives of mine—but the others I didn't know. Suddenly, I realized that all the ones I knew were people who had died.

One might well ask how to classify this experience, since it has points of similarity to both near-death and isolation experiences. It seems somewhat analogous to the near-death experiences in which meetings with the spirits of departed individuals took place, and yet different from them in that no other near-death phenomena took place. Interestingly, in one isolation study a subject, who was alone in a cubicle for some time, described hallucinations in which he saw pictures of famous men drifting past him. So, is the experience just quoted to be classified as a near-death experience occasioned by the patient's extreme illness, or as an isolation experience brought on by the conditions of confinement necessitated by the state of his health? It might even be the case that no absolute criteria can be drawn up which would enable one to classify every such experience into one of the two separate categories. Perhaps there will always be borderline cases.

Despite these overlaps, however, the results of isolation research do not provide a satisfactory explanation for near-death experiences. In the first place, the diverse mental phenomena occurring in conditions of isolation cannot themselves be explained by any current theory. To appeal to isolation studies to explain near-death experiences would be, as in the case of "explaining" out-of-body experiences by referring to autoscopic hallucinations, merely to substitute one mystery for another. For, there are two conflicting strains of thought about the nature of the visions which take place in conditions of isolation. Some no doubt take them as "unreal" and "hallucinatory," and yet all throughout history mystics and shamans have sought solitude in the wilderness in order to find enlightenment and revelation. The notion that spiritual rebirth can be brought about by isolation is an integral part of the belief systems of many cultures and is reflected in many great religious writings, including *The Bible*.

Although this idea is somewhat alien to our contemporary Western belief structure, there are still numerous proponents of it, even in our own society. One of the earliest and most influential isolation researchers, John Lilly, M.D., has recently written a book, a spiritual autobiography, entitled *The Center of the Cyclone*. In this book he makes it clear that he regards the experiences he had under conditions of isolation to be real experiences of enlightenment and insight, and not "unreal" or "delusional" at all. It is also interesting to note that he recounts a near-death experience of his own which is very much like the ones with which I have dealt, and that he puts his near-death experiences in the same category with his isolation experiences. Isolation, therefore, may very well be, along with hallucinatory drugs and a close call with death, one of several ways of entering new realms of consciousness.

2. DREAMS, HALLUCINATIONS, AND DELUSIONS

Perhaps, some say, near-death experiences are only wish-fulfilling dreams, fantasies, or hallucinations which are brought into play by different factors—drugs in one case, cerebral anoxia in another, isolation in yet another, and so on. So, they would explain near-death experiences as delusions.

I think several factors weigh against this. First, consider the great similarity in content and progression we find among the descriptions, despite the fact that what is most generally reported is manifestly not what is commonly imagined, in our cultural milieu, to happen to the dead. In addition, we find that the picture of the events of dying which emerges from these accounts corresponds in a striking way with that painted in very ancient and esoteric writings totally unfamiliar to my subjects.

Secondly, there remains the fact that the persons with whom I have talked are not victims of psychoses. They have struck me as emotionally stable, normal people who are functional in society. They hold jobs and positions of importance and carry them out responsibly. They have stable marriages and are involved with their families and friends. Almost no one with whom I have talked has had more than one uncanny experience in the course of his life. And, most significantly, these informants are people who can distinguish between dreams and waking experience.

Yet, they are people who report what they underwent as they came near death, not as dreams, but as events which happened to them. They almost invariably assure me in the course of their narratives that their experiences were not dreams, but rather were definitely, emphatically real.

Finally, there is the fact that independent corroboration of a kind exists for certain of the reports of out-of-body episodes. Though commitments to others prevent me from giving names and identifying details, I have seen and heard enough to say that I continue to be baffled and amazed. It is my opinion that anyone looking into near-death experiences in an organized way is likely also to uncover such strange apparent corroboration. At least, I believe he will find enough facts to make him wonder whether near-death experiences, far from being dreams, might not belong in a very different category indeed.

As a final note here, let me point out that "explanations" are not abstract intellectual systems. They are also in some respects products of the egos of the persons who hold them. People become emotionally wedded, as it were, to the canons of scientific explanation which they devise or adopt.

In numerous lectures on my collection of narratives of near-death events, I have encountered proponents of many types of explanations. Persons who are physiologically-, pharmacologically-, or neurologically-minded will regard their own orientations as sources of explanations which are intuitively obvious, even when cases are brought up which seem to weigh against that particular explanation. Those who espouse the theories of Freud delight in seeing the being of light as a projection of the subject's father, while Jungians see archetypes of the collective unconscious, and so on *ad infinitum*.

Although I want to emphasize again that I am not proposing any new explanations of my own through all this, I have tried to give a few reasons why explanations that are often proposed seem to me at least questionable. In fact, all I really want to suggest is this: Let us at least leave open the possibility that near-death experiences represent a novel phenomenon for which we may have to devise new modes of explanation and interpretation.

VI.
IMPRESSIONS

In writing this book I have been acutely conscious that my purpose and perspectives might very easily be misunderstood. In particular, I would like to say to scientifically-minded readers that I am fully aware that what I have done here does not constitute a scientific study. And to my fellow philosophers I would insist that I am not under the the delusion that I have "proven" there is life after death. To deal with these matters thoroughly would involve the discussion of technical details which lie beyond the scope of this book, so I shall limit myself to the following brief remarks.

In such specialized studies as logic, law, and science the words "conclusion," "evidence," and "proof" are technical terms and have more sophisticated meanings than they do in common usage. In everyday language these same words are used very loosely. A glance at any of the more sensational popular magazines will enable one to see that almost any unlikely tale will be given as "proof" of some improbable claim.

In logic what can and cannot be said to follow from a given set of premises is not at all a casual matter. It is very vigorously and precisely defined by rules, conventions, and laws. When one says that one has drawn a certain "conclusion," one is implicitly making the claim that anyone who begins from the same premises must arrive at the same conclusion, unless he has made a mistake in logic.

These remarks indicate why I refuse to draw any "conclusions" from my study and why I say that I am not trying to construct a proof of the ancient doctrine of the survival of bodily death. Yet I think that these reports of near-death experiences are very significant. What I want to do is find some middle way of interpreting them—a way which neither rejects these experiences on the basis that they do not constitute scientific or logical proof nor sensationalizes them by resorting to vague emotional claims that they "prove" that there is life after death.

At the same time, it seems to me to be an open possibility that our present inability to construct a "proof" may not represent a limitation imposed by the nature of the near-death experiences themselves. Perhaps it is instead a limitation of the currently accepted modes of scientific and logical thought. It may be that the perspective of scientists and logicians of the future will be very different. (One must remember that historically logic and scientific methodology have not been fixed and static systems but growing, dynamic processes.)

So I am left, not with conclusions or evidence or proofs, but with something much less definite—feelings, questions, analogies, puzzling facts to be explained. In fact, it might be more appropriate to ask, not what conclusions I have drawn on the basis of my study, but rather how the study has affected me personally. In response I can only say: There is something very persuasive about seeing a person describe his experience which cannot easily be conveyed in writing. Their near-death experiences were very real events to these people, and through my association with them the experiences have become real events to me.

I realize, however, that this is a psychological consideration and not a logical one. Logic is a public matter, and psychological considerations are not public in the same way. One person may be affected or changed in one way and another person in a different way by the same set of circumstances. It is a matter of disposition and temperament, and I do no wish to imply that my own reaction to this study should be a law for the thinking of everyone else. In view of this, some might ask, "If the interpretation of these experiences is ultimately such a subjective matter, why study them?" I can think of no other way to answer this than to point again to the universal human concern with the nature of death. I believe that any light whatever which can be shed on the nature of death is to the good.

Enlightenment on this subject is needed by members of many professions and academic fields. It is needed by the physician who has to deal with the fears and hopes of the dying patient and by the minister helping others to face death. It is needed also by psychologists and psychiatrists, because in order to devise a workable and reliable method for the therapy of emotional disturbances they need to know what the mind *is* and whether it can exist apart from the body. If it cannot, then the emphasis of psychological therapy would shift ultimately toward physical methods—drugs, electric shock therapy, brain surgery, and the like. On the other hand, if there are indications that the mind can exist apart from the body and that it is something in its own right, then therapy for mental disorders must finally be something very different.

However, more than academic and professional issues are involved. It involves deeply personal issues, for what we learn about death may make an important difference in the way we live our lives. If experiences of the type which I have discussed are real, they have very profound implications for what every one of us is doing with his life. For, then it would be true that we cannot fully understand this life until we catch a glimpse of what lies beyond it.

BIBLIOGRAPHY

EVANS-WENTZ, W. Y. (ed.), *The Tibetan Book of the Dead*, New York, Oxford University Press, 1957.

HAMILTON, EDITH and CAIRNS, HUNTINGTON (eds.), *The Collected Dialogues of Plato*, New York, Bollingen Foundation, 1961.

LILLY, JOHN C., M.D., *The Center of the Cyclone*, New York, The Julian Press, 1972.

LUKIANOWICZ, N., "Autoscopic Hallucinations," *Archives of Neurology and Psychiatry* (August, 1958).

PLATO, *The Last Days of Socrates*, trans. by Hugh Tredennick, Baltimore, Penguin Books, 1959.

STEVENSON, IAN, M.D., *Twenty Cases Suggestive of Reincarnation*, Charlottesville, University Press of Virginia, 1974.

SWEDENBORG, EMANUEL, *Compendium of the Theological and Spiritual Writings of Emanuel Swedenborg*, Boston, Crosby and Nichols, 1853.

WEIL, ANDREW, M.D., *The Natural Mind*, Boston, Houghton Mifflin, 1973.

Reflections on Life After Life

by Raymond A. Moody, Jr.

With Love
for Elisabeth, who has helped us see the way
and for Vi, Andy, and Dannion, three who came back

Acknowledgments

T his book was in preparation for a period of well over a year, and in that time many people and institutions have aided me in conceiving and planning it. First of all, I would like to thank the many hundreds of people who have told or written me of their spiritual experiences as they faced imminent death. The comments, questions, suggestions, and references to related literature which so many people have so kindly taken the time to write to me have been greatly appreciated.

Elisabeth Kübler-Ross, M.D., has given encouragement to go on with the work of discussing with persons their close calls with death. Ian Stevenson, M.D., has helped by reviewing and commenting on the section on methodology. George Ritchie, M.D., read the manuscript and made valuable remarks, even at a time when he was busy, not only with his own practice, but also with the task of writing a book about his own experience. Beverley Belk, M.D., has drawn upon her own practical wisdom and clinical acumen to make many interesting suggestions about how studies of this phenomenon might be carried out. John Audette spent considerable time in the library finding literature on the subject of this book, and in preparing a bibliography.

Very special thanks go to John Egle of Mockingbird Books, for helping in ways too numerous to list. Last but not least, I want to express my appreciation to my wife, Louise, and my two sons, for everything they have done in the way of making this volume possible.

———————

Abraham saith unto him, "They have Moses and the prophets; let them hear them." And he said, "Nay, father Abraham; but if one went unto them from the dead, they will repent." And he said unto him, "If they hear not Moses and the prophets, neither will they be persuaded, though one rose from the dead."   *Luke 16: 29-31*

Strange, is it not? that of the
        myriads who
Before us passed the door of
        Darkness through,
Not one returns to tell us of the
        Road,
Which to discover we must
        travel too.

                     Omar Khayyam

CONTENTS

Introduction

The present volume, which is intended to be read in conjunction with my previous book, *Life After Life*, represents an extension of and an addition to some of the concepts and findings discussed there.

Since the publication of *Life After Life*, I have had the opportunity to interview many more people who have had near-death experiences. As a matter of fact, I am now uncovering new cases of this phenomenon so rapidly that I am no longer keeping track of the exact number. As in my previous study, some of these people were actually pronounced clinically dead, while others only came very close to death in the course of a serious injury or accident. In the mass of material which has resulted, the fifteen common elements discussed in *Life After Life* have continued to recur. In addition, I have encountered some new and unusual experiences which seem to expand the list of elements.

For years I had wondered why, if these experiences *were* as common as I had found them to be, other people weren't also collecting reports of them. I felt that when I reported on my research, it might be thought that I was fabricating all this. Indeed, it even occurred to me that maybe this was not a widespread phenomenon, that perhaps, by some wild chain of coincidences, I had stumbled upon the *only* cases of this experience which there were or ever would be. This was a frightening thought to me in that in writing *Life After Life* I was banking heavily on a kind of repeatability—that is, that any sympathetic and diligent investigator could find an ample number of cases for himself.

Interestingly, many recent developments have settled a lot of my anxiety about this. I have found that several other physicians—most notably Dr. Elisabeth Kübler-Ross—have been pursuing this same research and have been getting identical accounts. In fact, when Dr. Kübler-Ross received pre-publication proofs on my first book, she wrote my publisher that she could have written the same manuscript herself on the basis of what she had been doing. She states that she now has hundreds of reports of this kind, and she is in the process of preparing a major book on the subject. Numerous doctors and ministers have also told me that they had long been noticing isolated cases of this phenomenon and felt that it might be quite prevalent.

When I gave talks on this subject in the past, individuals who had experienced near-death phenomena came forward only privately afterward. However, I have noticed in recent months a new openness and willingness to talk. Some people have now been relating their experiences publicly and unsolicitedly during the discussion periods which follow my lectures. Thus, many others have now had the experience of actually hearing firsthand from people who have been close to death and of sensing something of the warmth and sincerity that I have found in these accounts.

On the basis of these and many other similar developments,

I can now say with confidence that this phenomenon—whatever it ultimately means—*is* a widespread one. Indeed, it is so widespread that I believe that very soon the question will not be whether there really is such a phenomenon but rather, "What are we to make of it?" One of the points of *Life After Life* was simply to introduce the phenomenon and to predict that if others were interested, they, too, could find instances of it. It now appears that many others are interested in studying near-death experiences.

As a beginning, then, to this new volume, let me restate the theoretically complete model experience which I first constructed in *Life After Life*. It embodies all of the common elements of typical near-death experiences.

A man is dying and, as he reaches the point of greatest physical distress, he hears himself pronounced dead by his doctor. He begins to hear an uncomfortable noise, a loud ringing or buzzing, and at the same time feels himself moving very rapidly through a long tunnel. After this, he suddenly finds himself outside of his own physical body, but still in the immediate physical environment, and he sees his own body from a distance, as though he is a spectator. He watches the resuscitation attempt from this unusual vantage point and is in a state of emotional upheaval.

After a while, he collects himself and becomes more accustomed to his odd condition. He notices that he still has a "body," but one of a very different nature and with very different powers from the physical body he has left behind. Soon other things begin to happen. Others come to meet and to help him. He glimpses the spirits of relatives and friends who have already died, and a loving, warm spirit of a kind he has never encountered before—a being of light—appears before him. This being asks him a question non-verbally, to make him evaluate his life and helps him along by showing him a panoramic, instantaneous playback of the major events of his life. At some point he finds himself approaching some sort of barrier or border, apparently representing the limit between earthly life and the next life. Yet, he finds that he must go back to the earth, that the time for his death has not yet come. At this point he resists, for by now he is taken up with his experiences in the afterlife and does not want to return. He is overwhelmed by intense feelings of joy, love, and peace. Despite his attitude, though he somehow reunites with his physical body and lives.

Later he tries to tell others, but he has trouble doing so. In the first place, he can find no human words adequate to describe these unearthly episodes. He also finds that others scoff, so he stops telling other people. Still, the experience affects his life profoundly, especially his views about death and its relationship to life.

I.
NEW ELEMENTS

In the process of studying the large number of accounts of near-death experiences which I have collected since the completion of *Life After Life*, I have encountered several new elements which were not included there. Each of the elements I will discuss in this chapter has been reported to me by more than one person, but they are far from being as common as the original fifteen. With the exception of the "supernatural rescues," all of these unusual elements occurred exclusively in the reports of subjects who had near-death encounters of extreme duration.

The Vision of Knowledge

Several people have told me that during their encounters

with "death," they got brief glimpses of an entire separate realm of existence in which all knowledge—whether of past, present, or future—seemed to co-exist in a sort of timeless state. Alternately, this has been described as a moment of enlightenment in which the subject seemed to have complete knowledge. In trying to talk about this aspect of their experience, all have commented that this experience was ultimately inexpressible. Also, all agree that this feeling of complete knowledge did not persist after their return; that they did not bring back any sort of omniscience. They agree that this vision did not discourage them from trying to learn in this life, but, rather, encouraged them to do so.

The experience has been compared, in various accounts, to a flash of universal insight, institutions of higher learning, a "school," and a "library." Everyone emphasizes, however, that the words they are using to describe this experience are at best only dim reflections of the reality they are trying to express. It is my own feeling that there may be one underlying state of consciousness which is at the root of all these different accounts.

One woman who had "died" gave the following report during an extended interview.

You mentioned earlier that you seemed to have "a vision of knowledge," if I could call it that. Could you tell me about it?

This seems to have taken place after I had seen my life pass before me. It seemed that all of a sudden, all knowledge—of all that had started from the very beginning, that would go on without end—that for a second I knew all the secrets of all ages, all the meaning of the universe, the stars, the moon—of everything. But after I chose to return, this knowledge escaped, and I can't remember any of it. It seems that when I made the decision [to return] I was told that I would not retain the knowledge. But I kept being called back by my children. . . .

This all-powerful knowledge opened before me. It

seemed that I was being told that I was going to remain sick for quite a while and that I would have other close calls. And I did have several close calls after that. They said some of it would be to erase this all-knowing knowledge that I had picked up . . . that I had been granted the universal secrets and that I would have to undergo time to forget that knowledge. But I do have the memory of once knowing everything, that it did happen, but that it was not a gift that I would keep if I returned. But I chose to return to my children. . . . The memory of all these things that happened has remained clear, all except for that fleeting moment of knowledge. And that feeling of all knowledge disappeared when I returned to my body.

It sounds silly! Well, it does when you say it out loud . . . or it does to me, because I've never been able to sit and talk to someone else about it.

I don't know how to explain it but I knew. . . . As *The Bible* says, "To you all things will be revealed." For a minute there was no question that didn't have an answer. How long I knew it, I couldn't say. It wasn't in earthly time, anyway.

In what form did this knowledge seem to be presented to you? Was it in words or pictures?

It was in all forms of communication, sights, sounds, thoughts. It was any—and everything. It was as if there was nothing that wasn't known. All knowledge was there, not just of one field, but everything.

One thing I wonder. I've spent a lot of my life seeking knowledge, learning. If this happens, isn't that sort of thing rather pointless?

No! You still want to seek knowledge even after you come back here. I'm still seeking knowledge. . . . It's not silly to try to get the answers here. I sort of felt that it was part of our purpose . . . but that it wasn't just for one person, but that it was to be used for all mankind. We're always reaching out to help others with what we know.

There is one point which I would like to make here about this narrative. This woman plainly had the impression that part of the purpose of her lengthy recuperation was to make her forget almost all of the knowledge which had been revealed to her. This suggests that some mechanism was operative that had the function of blocking the knowledge acquired in this state of existence so that it could not be carried over into the physical state of being.

I am impressed by the similarity between this concept and one which was expressed—in an admittedly metaphorical and poetic way—by Plato in his telling of the story of Er, a warrior who came back to life on the funeral pyre, after having been believed dead. Er is said to have seen many things in the afterlife, but he was told that he must return to physical life to tell others what death is like. Just before he returned, he saw souls which were being prepared to be born into life:

> They all journeyed to the Plain of Oblivion, through a terrible and stifling heat, for it was bare of trees and all plants, and there they camped at eventide by the River of Forgetfulness, whose waters no vessel can contain. They were all required to drink a measure of the water, and those who were not saved by their good sense drank more than the measure, and each one as he drank forgot all things. And after they had fallen asleep and it was the middle of the night, there was a sound of thunder and a quaking of the earth, and they were suddenly wafted thence, one this way, one that, upward to their birth like shooting stars. Er himself, he said, was not allowed to drink of the water, yet how and in what way he returned to the body he said he did not know, but suddenly recovering his sight he saw himself at dawn lying on the funeral pyre.[1]

The basic theme being presented here, that before returning to life a certain kind of "forgetting" of knowledge one has in the

eternal state must take place, is similar in the two cases.
During another interview, a young man told me this:

Now, I was in a school . . . and it was real. It was not
imaginary. If I were not absolutely sure, I would say, "Well,
there is a possibility that I was in this place." But it *was*
real. It was like a school and there was no one there, and
yet there were a lot of people there. Because if you looked
around, you would *see* nothing . . . but if you paid attention, you would feel, sense, the presence of other beings
around. . . . It's as if there were lessons coming at me and
they would keep coming at me. . . .

*That's interesting. Another man told me that he went into
what he called "libraries" and "institutions of higher learning." Is that anything like what you're trying to tell me?*

Exactly! You see, hearing what you say he said about it,
it's like I know exactly what he means, that I know he's
been through this same thing I have. And, yet . . . the
words I would use are different, because there really are no
words . . . I cannot describe it. You could not compare it to
anything here. The terms I'm using to describe it are so far
from the thing, but it's the best I can do. . . . Because this
is a place where the *place* is knowledge. . . . Knowledge
and information are readily available—all knowledge. . . .
You absorb knowledge. . . . You all of a sudden know the
answers . . . It's like you focus mentally on one place in
that school and—zoom—knowledge flows by you from
that place, automatically. It's just like you'd had about a
dozen speed reading courses.
And I know verbatim what this man is talking about,
but, you see, I'm just putting the same consciousness into
my own words, which are different. . . .
I go on seeking knowledge; "Seek and ye shall find." You
can get the knowledge for yourself. But I *pray* for wisdom,
wisdom more than all. . . .

A middle-aged lady described it this way:

There was a moment in this thing—well, there isn't any way to describe it—but it was like I knew all things. . . . For a moment, there, it was like communication wasn't necessary. I thought whatever I wanted to know could be known.

Cities of Light

I stated in *Life After Life* that I had not found any cases in which a "heaven"—at least in a certain traditional portrayal of that place—was described. However, I have now talked with numerous individuals who tell with remarkable consistency of catching glimpses of other realms of being which might well be termed "heavenly." It is interesting to me that in several of these accounts a single phrase—"a city of light"—occurs. In this and several other respects the imagery in which these scenes are described seems to be reminiscent of what is found in *The Bible*.

One middle-aged man who had a cardiac arrest related:

I had heart failure and clinically died. . . . I remember everything perfectly vividly. . . . Suddenly I felt numb. Sounds began sounding a little distant. . . . All this time I was perfectly conscious of everything that was going on. I heard the heart monitor go off. I saw the nurse come into the room and dial the telephone, and the doctors, nurses, and attendants came in.

As things began to fade there was a sound I can't describe; it was like the beat of a snare drum, very rapid, a rushing sound, like a stream rushing through a gorge. And I rose up and I was a few feet up looking down on my body. There I was, with people working on me. I had no fear. No pain. Just peace. After just probably a second or two, I seemed to turn over and go up. It was dark—you could call it a hole or a tunnel—and there was this bright light. It got brighter and brighter. And I seemed to go *through* it.

All of a sudden I was just somewhere else. There was a gold-looking light, everywhere. Beautiful. I couldn't find a source anywhere. It was just all around, coming from everywhere. There was music. And I seemed to be in a countryside with streams, grass, and trees, mountains. But when I looked around—if you want to put it that way— they were not trees and things like we know them to be. The strangest thing to me about it was that there were people there. Not in any kind of form or body as we know it; they were just there.

There was a sense of perfect peace and contentment; love. It was like I was part of it. That experience could have lasted the whole night or just a second . . . I don't know.

Here's the way one woman described it:

There was a vibration of some sort. The vibration was surrounding me, all around my body. It was like the body vibrating, and where the vibration came from, I don't know. But when it vibrated, I became separated. I could then see my body. . . . I stayed around for a while and watched the doctor and nurses working on my body, wondering what would happen. . . . I was at the head of the bed, looking at them and my body, and at one time one nurse reached up to the wall over the bed to get the oxygen mask that was there and as she did she reached *through* my neck. . . .

And after I floated up, I went through this dark tunnel . . . I went into the black tunnel and came out into brilliant light. . . . A little bit later on I was there with my grandparents and my father and my brother, who had died. . . . There was the most beautiful, brilliant light all around. And this was a beautiful place. There were colors—bright colors—not like here on earth, but just indescribable. There were people there, happy people. . . . People were around, some of them gathered in groups. Some of them were learning. . . .

Off in the distance . . . I could see a city. There were buildings—separate buildings. They were gleaming, bright. People were happy in there. There was sparkling water, fountains . . . a city of light I guess would be the way to say it. . . . It was wonderful. There was beautiful music. Everything was just glowing, wonderful. . . . But if I had entered into this, I think I would never have returned. . . . I was told that if I went there I couldn't go back . . . that the decision was mine.

An elderly man said:

I was sitting in a chair. I started to get up and something hit me right in the chest. . . . I leaned against the wall. I sat down again, and then it hit me again, just like a sledge hammer hit me in the chest. . . . I was in the hospital . . . and they said I had a cardiac arrest. The doctor was right there.

And what do you remember of your cardiac arrest?

Well, it's a place . . . It's really beautiful, but you just can't describe it. But it's really there. You just can't imagine it. When you get on the other side, there's a river. Just like in *The Bible*, "There is a river. . . ." It had a smooth surface, just like glass. . . ." Yeah, you cross a river. I did. . . .

How did you feel you crossed this river?

Walked. Just walked. But it was so pretty. It's beautiful. There's no way to describe it. We have beauty here, there's no question, with all these flowers and everything. But there is no comparison. It's so quiet over there and so peaceful . . . You feel like just resting. There was no darkness.

A Realm of Bewildered Spirits

Several people have reported to me that at some point they glimpsed other beings who seemed to be "trapped" in an apparently most unfortunate state of existence. Those who described seeing these confused beings are in agreement on several points. First, they state that these beings seemed to be, in effect, unable to surrender their attachments to the physical world. One man recounted that the spirits he saw apparently "couldn't progress on the other side because their god is still living here." That is, they seemed bound to some particular object, person, or habit. Secondly, all have remarked that these beings appeared "dulled," that their consciousness seemed somehow limited in contrast with that of others. Thirdly, they say it appeared that these "dulled spirits" were to be there only until they solved whatever problem or difficulty was keeping them in that perplexed state.

These points of agreement come across in the following segment of an interview with one woman who was believed "dead" for some fifteen minutes.

You mentioned seeing these people–spirits who seemed very confused. Could you tell me more about them?

These bewildered people? I don't know exactly where I saw them. . . . But as I was going by, there was this area that was dull—this is in contrast to all the brilliant light. The figures were more humanized than the rest of them were, if you stop to think of it in that respect, but neither were they in quite human form as we are.

What you would think of as their head was bent downward; they had sad, depressed looks, they seemed to shuffle, as someone would on a chain gang. I don't know why I say this because I don't remember noticing feet. I don't know what they were, but they looked washed out, dull, gray. And they seemed to be forever shuffling and moving around, not knowing where they were going, not knowing who to follow, or what to look for.

As I went by they didn't even raise their heads to see what was happening. They seemed to be thinking, "Well, it's all over with. What am I doing? What's it all about?" Just this absolute, crushed, hopeless demeanor—not knowing what to do or where to go or who they were or anything else.

They seemed to be forever moving, rather than just sitting, but in no special direction. They would start straight, then veer to the left and take a few steps and veer back to the right. And absolutely nothing to do. Searching, but for what they were searching I don't know.

Did they seem to be aware of the physical world?

They didn't seem to be aware of anything—not the physical world or the spiritual world. They seemed to be caught in between somewhere. It's neither spiritual or physical. It's on a level somewhere between the two—or it appeared so to me. They may have some contact with the physical world. Something is tying them down, because they all seemed to be bent over and looking downward, maybe into the physical world . . . maybe watching something they hadn't done or should do. They couldn't make up their minds what to do, because they all had the most woebegone expressions; there was no color of life.

So they seemed to be bewildered?

Very bewildered; not knowing who they are or what they are. It looks like they have lost any knowledge of who they are, what they are—no identity whatsoever.

Would you say they were in between the physical world and what you were in?

In my memory, what I saw was after I left the physical hospital. As I said, I felt I rose upward and it was between, it was *before* I actually entered this tunnel—as I referred to it—and before I entered the spiritual world where there is so much brilliant sunlight—well, not sunlight, but the brilliant light that surrounded everything and was brighter than sunlight, but it didn't hurt like the sunlight can hurt your eyes, no glare to it. But in this particular place there was the dullest, drab gray. Now, I have a friend who is color blind and I've heard him say that the world to him is just shades and tones of gray. But to me, I'm full of color—and this was something that was maybe like a black and white movie. Just the different tones of gray—dingy, washed out.

They were not aware of me. They showed no sign of being aware that I was there. It was quite depressing.

They seemed to be trying to decide; they were looking back; they didn't know whether to go on or to return to the bodies where they were. They did seem to hover; they kept looking downward and never upward. They didn't want to go on to see what was awaiting them; they also reminded me of what I have read of as descriptions of ghosts; they would be mainly the see-through type of thing. There seems to have been a great huge array of them around.

Some persons who have seen this phenomenon have noticed certain of these beings apparently trying unsuccessfully to communicate with persons who were still physically alive. One man related many instances he observed while he was "dead" for an extended period of time. For example, he told how he saw an ordinary man walking, unaware, down the street while one of these dulled spirits hovered above him. He said he had the feeling that this spirit had been, while alive, the man's mother, and, still unable to give up her earthly role, was trying to tell her son what to do. The following excerpt from an interview with a woman subject relates another example.

Could you see any of them trying to talk to other [phyiscal] people?

Un, huh. You could see them trying to make contact, but no one would realize that they were around; people would just ignore them. . . . They were trying to communicate, yet there was no way they could break through. People seemed to be completely unaware of them.

Could you tell anything they were trying to say?

One seemed to be a woman who was trying so hard to reach through to children and to an older woman in the house. I wondered if in some way this was the mother of the children, and maybe the daughter of the older woman in the house, and she was trying to break through to them. This seemed to me to be meaning that she was trying to reach the children and they continued to play and pay no attention, and the older person seemed to be going about in the kitchen doing work with no awareness that this person was around.

Was there any particular thing she was trying to tell them?

Well, it seems more or less that she was trying to get through to them, trying to tell them, seemingly, to do things differently from what they were doing now, to change, to make a change in their life style. Now, this sounds kind of put on, but she was trying to get them to do the right things, to change so as not to be left like she was. "Don't do as I did, so this won't happen to you. Do things for others so that you won't be left like this."

I'm not trying to moralize or make a sermon, but this seemed to be the message that she was trying to get across. . . . It seemed that in this house there was no love, if you want to put it that way. . . . It seemed that she was trying to atone for something she had done. . . . It's an experience I'll never forget.

Supernatural Rescues

In several accounts I have collected, persons say that they had near-death experiences through which they were saved from physical death by the interposition of some spiritual agent or being. In each case, the person involved found himself (knowingly or unknowingly) in a potentially fatal accident or set of circumstances from which it was beyond his own powers to escape. He may even have given up and prepared himself to die. However, at this point a voice or a light manifested itself and rescued him from the brink of death. Persons undergoing this relate that afterward their lives were changed, that they came to feel they were saved from death for a purpose. They have all reported that their religious beliefs were strengthened.

One experience of this type which has become quite well known is that related in the book *A Man Called Peter*, by Catherine Marshall. She describes how, during his boyhood in Scotland, Peter Marshall was saved from falling to his death over a cliff in the fog by a voice which called to him from behind. This experience affected him greatly, and he went on to become a minister.

Here is a part of one interview in which a "rescue" of this type is reported. A man told me of being involved in an industrial accident in which he was trapped in a huge vat, into which a stream of very hot acid and steam was being pumped under high pressure. He recalled:

The heat of all this was terrific. I yelled, "Let me out of here. I'm getting trapped." I had gotten as far as I could into a corner, and put my face into the corner, but the stuff was so hot that it was burning me through my clothing. So, at that time I realized that in just a matter of minutes I would be scalded to death.

I guess it was in my weakness or whatever that I gave up. To myself, I just said, "This is it, I'm a goner." I could not see, and the heat was so intense that I could not open my eyes. I had my eyes closed the whole time. But it seemed that the whole area lit up with a glow. And a verse of Scripture that I had heard all my life, that had never meant too much to me, "Lo, I am with thee always," came from a direction which later turned out to be the only way out.

I couldn't stand to open my eyes, but I could still see the light, so I followed it. I know that my eyes were closed the whole time, though. The doctor didn't even treat my eyes later. No acid got in them. . . .

Did this change your life in any way?

After I got back to work, some of the people who work there were talking about how calm I was after the whole thing had happened. I'm not that brave a man; I don't have that much courage. The fact that I was lead by an unseen hand out of the danger was the source of my courage, was the calmness they saw. It was not in me. The voice that led me out was the same voice that gave me that courage.

I know that the hand of Jesus Christ reached down and got me out of that place. I think it's not a matter of think, it's a matter of *know* that it was God's will that my life be spared—for what reason, I don't know. At that time I was not living as close to God as I should have. I have been drawn closer to him by this. I still have problems. I know that a God that can step in and save a man in a moment of crisis can handle anything. So I have learned to depend on him.

When you heard the voice, was it just like a normal physical voice?

No. It was as if it was magnified, amplified. There was no question that I heard. There was no question as to the direction it came from. If it had come from my right or from my left, and I had followed it, I would have been instantly killed. The fact that it came from the direction it came from and that I followed the voice was why I came out alive. . . .

Never would I have stepped out into that heat myself. I knew what I was in for.

[This voice] was a commanding voice—not "Will you come this way?" The first thing that popped into my mind was "Here I am down here by myself and I'm going to die." And when I heard that voice, there was no doubt in my mind, I knew that within myself I had no way to get out.

How long did this last?

It seemed like an eternity. In other words if you are crawling some forty or fifty feet through acid, each time you make a move you know you are moving at top speed. I would say the whole thing happened in a matter of a couple or three minutes after I saw that I was trapped, but it seemed like an eternity.

Did this seem like a normal physical light?

No. It was nothing like I had ever seen before. It was what you might see if you looked up into the sunlight. And this was a dark place where I was trapped. It was a big bright light and a voice. I didn't see a figure or anything like that. I followed the light the whole way.

Did the light seem to hurt your eyes? Was it uncomfortable to look into it?

No. Not in any way.

Did it seem to have any particular color?

No. Nothing other than just a bright white light. It was like the sun—like looking into the sun.

Another man reported:

This was during World War II . . . and I was serving in

the infantry in Europe. I had an experience I won't ever forget. . . . I saw an enemy plane diving toward the building we were in, and it had opened fire on us. . . . The dust from the bullets was headed in a path right toward us. I was very scared and thought we would all be killed.

I didn't see a thing, but I felt a wonderful, comforting presence there with me, and a kind, gentle voice said, "I'm here with you, Reid. Your time has not come yet." I was so relaxed and comfortable in that presence. . . . Since that day, I have not been one bit afraid of death.

Finally, here is the account of one woman who was extremely ill with an infection. Note that in this example the patient seems to have been instructed and guided in her own resuscitation.

> The doctors had all given up on me. They said I was dying. . . . I got to the point where I was feeling the life going out of my body. . . . I could still hear what everyone was saying, though I couldn't see anything. I wished I could live to raise my children and to play a part in their lives. . . .
>
> That's when I heard God's voice talking to me. He had the most loving gentle voice. . . . I know I wasn't out of my head, as some people might think. . . . I could hear the voices of the others in the room, in the background . . . but I could sense his voice, too, and it was so overwhelming. He told me that if I wanted to live, I was going to have to breathe . . . and so I did, and when I took that one breath, I started to come back. Then he told me to breathe again, and I was able to take another breath, and life came back into my body. . . .
>
> The doctors were amazed. They had all given me up, and naturally they hadn't heard the voice I had. They couldn't understand what happened.

I will close this chapter by reminding the reader that these are by no means common accounts of near-death experiences.

However, they have occurred in a sizeable number of my cases and each of them is connected, within the context of the particular experience, with the elements which were reported earlier. For example, in the first interview quoted under "The Vision of Knowledge" above, the subject also described being out of her body, going through a dark tunnel, seeing the events of her life in review, and many other of the common elements. Similarly, note that the passage through a dark tunnel and being out of the body are prominently reported in two of the interviews quoted above in "Cities of Light." In each case, these new features—like the ones with which I have previously dealt—were described to me by ordinary people, who were not seeking these experiences, who had no previous interest in or knowledge of such matters, and yet who, afterward, had absolutely no doubt about the reality of what they had seen.

[1] Edith Hamilton and Huntington Cairns, eds., *The Collected Dialogues of Plato*, trans. Hugh Tredennick, Bollingen Series 71 (New York: Pantheon Books, 1961), p.844.

II.
JUDGMENT

In discussing *Life After Life* one reviewer stated:

> The area sure to provoke controversy among religious groups is a section dealing with models of the afterlife. Most of the individuals interviewed did not experience any reward-punishment crisis—the traditional model of being reviewed by a St. Peter type before being admitted to the afterlife.[1]

Many people have brought up this point, so it seems appropriate to examine something in near-death experiences which may or may not, according to one's theology, be likened to the concept of a judgment. Again and again, my near-death subjects have described to me a panoramic, wrap-around, full-color, three-dimensional vision of the events of their lives. Some people say that during this vision they saw only the major events of their lives. Others go so far as to say that in the course of this panorama every single thing that they had ever done or thought was there for them to see. All the good things and all the bad were portrayed there at once, instantaneously. It will be remembered also that this panorama was quite frequently said to have taken place in the presence of a "being of light," whom some Christians identified as Christ, and that this being asked them a question, in effect, "What have you done with your life?"

In being pressed to explain as precisely as they can what the point of this question was, most people come up with something like the formulation of one man who put it to me most succinctly when he said that he was asked whether he had done the things he did *because* he loved others, that is, from the *motivation* of love. At this point, one might say, a kind of judgment took place, for in this state of heightened awareness, when people saw any selfish acts which they had done they felt extremely repentant. Likewise, when gazing upon those events in which they had shown love and kindness they felt satisfaction.

It is interesting to note that the judgment in the cases I studied came not from the being of light, who seemed to love and accept these people anyway, but rather from within the individual being judged. A passage in Matthew respecting judgment is of some significance in this regard. The King James Version of *The Bible* has the passage translated as follows (Matthew 7:1-2):

> Judge not, that ye be not judged. For with what judgment ye judge, ye shall be judged; and with what measure ye mete, it shall be measured to you again.

However, in *Today's English Version of the New Testament* (also published as *Good News for Modern Man*), the following translation is given:

Do not judge others, so that God will not judge you—
because God will judge you in the same way you judge
others, and he will apply to you the same rules you apply to
others.

I am not a Biblical scholar, so I cannot rule on which of these
translations is the more accurate. However, I find it very
interesting that, purely from the point of view of what my
near-death subjects reported experiencing, the first translation
would be more applicable—the judgment came from within
them. In this state, they seemed to have seen for themselves
what they should and shouldn't have done and to have judged
themselves accordingly.

In thinking about all this, it has occurred to me that a very
common theme of near-death experiences is the feeling of
being *exposed* in one way or another. From one point of view
we human beings can be characterized as creatures who spend
a great deal of our time hiding behind various masks. We seek
inner security through money or power; we try to make ourselves feel that we are better than others by priding ourselves
on our social class, the degree of our education, the color of
our skin, our money, our power, the beauty of our bodies, our
identification with a male or female role, etc. We adorn our
bodies with clothes; we hide our innermost thoughts and certain of our deeds from the knowledge or sight of others.

However, in the moments around the time of death all such
masks are necessarily dropped. Suddenly, the person finds his
every thought and deed portrayed in a three-dimensional,
full-color panorama. If he meets other beings he reports that
they know his every thought and vice versa. He finds that in
this state communication is not mediated through words, but
rather that thoughts are understood directly—to the point
where, as one man put it, "You're too embarrassed to be around
people who don't think the way you do."

The beauty of the physical body or the color of the skin can no
longer be a source of pride. Indeed, people do not have physical bodies any more. The only beauty which appears now has
nothing at all to do with body; it is whatever beauty there may

be in the soul. Sexual identity is dropped too; most people feel that they had no specific male or female identity while in this state. It is somehow natural, then, that in these final moments two qualities which distinctly pertain to the mind, namely love and knowledge, stand forth in prominent relief.

One other feature of this review which might be mentioned is that some report that in addition to their acts, they can see portrayed before them the consequences of their acts for others. As one man put it most graphically:

> I first was out of my body, above the building, and I could see my body lying there. Then I became aware of the light—just light—being all around me. Then it seemed there was a display all around me, and everything in my life just went by for review, you might say. I was really very, very ashamed of a lot of the things that I experienced because it seemed that I had a different knowledge, that the light was showing me what was wrong, what I did wrong. And it was very real.
>
> It seemed like this flashback, or memory, or whatever was directed primarily at ascertaining the extent of my life. It was like there was a judgment being made and then, all of a sudden, the light became dimmer, and there was a conversation, not in words, but in thoughts. When I would see something, when I would experience a past event, it was like I was seeing it through eyes with (I guess you would say) omnipotent knowledge, guiding me, and helping me to see.
>
> That's the part that has stuck with me, because it showed me not only what I had done but *even how what I had done had affected other people*. And it wasn't like I was looking at a movie projector because I could *feel* these things; there was feeling, and particularly since I was with this knowledge . . . I found out that not even your thoughts are lost . . . Every thought was there . . . Your thoughts are not lost . . .

This situation can be regarded as being most unpleasant

indeed, and it is no wonder that quite frequently people may come back from this feeling that they need to make a change in their lives. Consider the following passages taken from interviews with two men.

(1) I didn't tell anybody about my experience, but when I got back, I had this overwhelming, burning, consuming desire to do something for other people . . . I was so ashamed of all the things that I had done, or hadn't done, in my life. I felt like I had to do it, that it couldn't wait.

(2) When I got back from this, I had decided I'd better change. I was very repentant. I hadn't been satisfied with the life I had led up to then, so I wanted to start doing better.

Although many people continue to ask me whether anyone with whom I have talked has reported a hell, it remains true that in the mass of material I have collected no one has ever described to me a state like the archetypical hell. However, I might remark that I have never interviewed anyone who had been a real rounder prior to his close call. The people I interviewed have been normal, nice people. Such transgressions as they were guilty of had been minor—the sorts of things we have all done. So one would not expect that they would have been consigned to a fiery pit. Yet nothing I have encountered precludes the posibility of a hell.

Some people seem to be bothered by the fact that the being of light is reported in these near-death experiences to be so totally loving and forgiving and to love people despite their many shortcomings, which are there revealed so graphically before him. For my own part, I can only say that I love my children despite their faults and that I am certain I would continue to love them no matter what they might do.

Others seem dissatisfied because they apparently think that these experiences are inconsistent with the notion of a Final Judgment at the end of the world. I see no discrepancy here. Obviously, if anyone were to have come back from "death" reporting that he went through the Final Judgment, then his experience would have been mistaken. Since the end of the world has not yet taken place, any report of its having occurred during a near-death experience would be, in effect, a disconfirmation of the validity of that experience. There may well be a Final Judgment; near-death experiences in no way imply the contrary. Indeed, many of the persons whom I have interviewed have mentioned their belief that this will take place. It should be added, though, that they accept this on the basis of scriptural authority alone and did not derive it from anything they learned or foresaw while in their state of near or apparent "death."

Notions of heaven and hell, judgment, the Final Judgment, the end of the world, and God's grace are all eschatological concepts which form the basis for much debate among theologians. They are all so ultimate, so cosmic in their importance that it is very hard for us human beings to talk about them directly, in mere human language. Hence, they have sometimes been portrayed in more picturesque, figurative terms.

As one goes through the history of painting in Europe, the concept of the judgment is portrayed at various ages through the use of such symbols as a record book or an account book, a court of law, and scales (the weighing out of souls). Plato, in his myth of Er, talks about the "markers" that souls which are facing judgment wear. In the *Tibetan Book of the Dead* the concept is portrayed as a "mirror of Karma." Remember that all along my near-death subjects have told me that the words they use to describe their experiences are only analogies or metaphors used to indicate experiences which ultimately lie beyond all human language. It is somehow not surprising, then, that the particular words used in our technological age are drawn from such contexts as the science of optics, as when the word "images" was used, or from technological developments such as slides or movies, and that these days and symbolism used almost reminds one of some of the more fantastic developments in the science of photography or in television technology; of the three-dimensional hologram or of the instant replay.

One final remark, with respect to the question of what might happen to persons such as the perpetrators of the Nazi horrors. If what my subjects have reported happens to everybody, imagine for a moment what would happen to them during this review, especially if, as some say, they see not only their selfish acts but also the consequences of those acts for others. Those who engineered the Nazi atrocities seem to have been people whose lack of love was so complete that they willed the deaths of millions of innocent persons. This resulted in countless individual tragedies of separation of parent from child, of husband from wife, of friend from friend. It resulted in innumerable long, lingering deaths and fast brutal ones. It resulted in awful degradations, in years of hunger, tears, and torment for their victims. If what happened to my subjects happened to these men, they would see all these things and many others come alive, vividly portrayed before them. In my wildest fantasies, I am totally unable to imagine a hell more horrible, more ultimately unbearable than this.

[1]Frederic A. Brussat, review of *Life After Life* in *Cultural Information Service*, Nov. 1976, pp. 16-17.

III.
SUICIDE

The term "suicide" is used in connection with a wide variety of at least potentially self-destructive behaviors which stem from many different apparent motives or conditions and which manifest themselves under widely varying circumstances. For many centuries mankind has been grappling with the many implications of suicidal behavior. At first it was approached from the theological, ethical, and philosophical points of view. In more recent times sociological and psychological perspectives have been added. Despite this long probing, many puzzling questions remain.

Given the fact that some people who have been revived from very close encounters with death have reported spiritual experiences, some have asked how these reports bear on the issue of suicide. The first thing that one must point out is that consideration of near-death experiences does not give us final answers to the many different kinds of puzzles we have about suicide. All we can do is address ourselves to two questions. First: Do persons who have had near-death experiences from causes other than suicidal attempts come back with any particular attitude toward suicide? And second: Do reported near-death experiences which resulted from suicidal attempts differ in any way from those which had other causes?

While people who have reported near-death experiences state quite often that they felt they did not want to come back from "death," nonetheless they all disavow suicide as a means of returning to this state. They come back saying that they feel they have learned in the course of their experience that they have a purpose to fulfill here in life. They return with a serious, dedicated attitude toward life and living. Absolutely no one that I have interviewed has sought a repeat performance of their experience.

Numerous people who had "died" of natural or accidental causes have told me that while they were in this state, it had been intimated to them that suicide was a very unfortunate act which was attended with a penalty. For example, one man who "died" after an accident told me:

> [While I was over there] I got the feeling that two things it would be completely forbidden for me to do would be to kill myself or to kill another person . . . If I were to commit suicide I would be throwing God's gift back in his face . . . Killing somebody else would be interfering with God's purpose for that individual.

Another man who survived an apparent clinical death of some duration said that while he was "over there" he had the impression that there was a "penalty" to pay for some acts of suicide, and that part of this would be to witness the suffering on the part of others that this act would cause.

At the time I completed the manuscript of my first book I had encountered very few significant cases of near-death resulting from attempted suicide. I think this is understandable in that persons who have had such experiences might be more reluctant to talk about them because of possible residual guilt feelings about the attempt. Since that time, however, I have come upon some additional cases. All of these people agree on one point: they felt their suicidal attempts solved nothing. They found that they were involved in exactly the same problem from which they had been trying to extricate themselves by suicide. Whatever difficulty they had been trying to get away from was still there on the other side, unresolved.

One person mention d being "trapped" in the situation which had provoked her suicide attempt. She had the feeling that the state of affairs in which she had been before her "death" was being repeated again and again, as if in a cycle.

This problem I was telling you about, you know, well, looking back on it now, of course, it doesn't seem so important, from a more adult way of looking at it. But at the time, as I was a person at that age, it really seemed very important . . . Well, the thing was, it was still around, even when I was "dead." And it was like it was repeating itself, a rerun. I would go through it once and at the end I would think, "Oh, I'm glad that's over," and then it would start all over again, and I would think, "Oh, no, not this again."

All mentioned that after their experiences, they would never consider trying suicide again. Their common attitude is that they had made a mistake, and that they were very glad they had not succeeded in their attempts. For instance, when I asked one man whether, in the light of what he had experienced, he would ever again choose to try to kill himself, he answered:

No. I would not do that again. I will die naturally next time, because one thing I realized at that time is that our life here is just such a small period of time and there is so much which needs to be done while you're here. And, when you die it's eternity.

It is quite interesting that the views and experiences outlined above coincide so closely with the sentiments expressed in a certain very ancient theological argument against suicide. Many diverse theologians and philosophers over the ages have argued against suicide from the premise that we are in life, in effect, on assignment or "as a gift" from God, and that it is just not our option to take our own lives. Thus Plato, in the *Phaedo*, alludes to the doctrine that we are placed on earth in a sort of post, and that we must not run away from it. He argues that, in essence, we belong to and are in the care of God and must not try to release ourselves in this way.[1] In the Middle Ages, Thomas Aquinas propounded the argument that since life is a kind of gift from God to man, it is up to God alone to make the judgment as to when it should end.[2] John Locke, the seventeenth-century British philosopher to whom we owe some of the ideas in the Declaration of Independence and the Constitution, declared, too, that we are the property of God and are placed here on his business, not to quit our stations willfully.[3]

Likewise, the German philosopher Immanuel Kant, a very different thinker indeed from the others, wrote:

> . . . as soon as we examine suicide from the standpoint of religion we immediately see it in its true light. We have been placed in this world under certain conditions and for specific purposes. But a suicide opposes the purpose of his creator; he arrives in the other world as one who has deserted his post; he must be looked upon as a rebel against God . . . God is our owner; we are his property; his providence works for our good.[4]

I do not present the above arguments to endorse their reasoning or to make an ethical or moral judgment about suicide. My only point is to suggest that much the same feelings about man's purpose in life and how that relates to the problem of suicide are expressed both in these theological arguments and in the words and thoughts of people who have had near-death experiences.

I realize that the experiences I have quoted in this chapter raise many questions. Some have pointed out that in certain cultures suicide is not morally condemned, as it generally is in our own. It may even be regarded as an honorable act, as in the case of Japan during the age of the samurai. One may ask, "Would a person from such a society report the same kind of experiences upon resuscitation from a suicidal 'death'?"

Further, some have suggested that, in effect, we are all committing suicide in one way or another. That is, most of us probably engage in some sort of activity which—we should know—will eventually harm us or cause our deaths. Three examples which are striking in our own society are smoking cigarettes, eating foods which have high levels of cholesterol, and driving under the influence of alcohol. People go right on doing these things despite their full knowledge that these actions could eventually result in death from any one of several diseases or from an automobile wreck. What is the difference, one might ask, between such behavior and "real" suicide? At what point on the spectrum of potentially self-destructive behavior would the "penalties" mentioned by the subjects quoted above begin to take effect?

Some persons commit suicide for altruistic reasons, to save others, for example. What would people who undergo such "heroic" deaths experience? Or what of persons who take their own lives in the throes of psychotic depression or horrendous loss?

It is also a well known fact that many who "attempt" suicide do not really intend to kill themselves, but are merely trying to draw the attention of others to their needs or problems in a dramatic way. Conversely, many psychiatrists hold that so-called accident-prone individuals, while they have no conscious desire to kill themselves, nonetheless *subconsciously* wish to do so. In this explanation, their apparent accidents would be unconscious suicidal attempts.

Obviously, no one has the final answers to such complex questions, and I am not trying to oversimplify these issues. All I can do is to report that the near-death experiences of which I am aware that took place in association with attempted suicides were different from others in the ways described.

When asked about such matters, a psychiatrist friend of mine, who had an "other-world" experience during an apparent clinical death from an infection, gave an interesting answer. He expressed the belief that God, in his nature, is much more forgiving, understanding, and just than we as humans are able to comprehend, and that God will take care of these things in accordance with his love and wisdom. What a suicidal person needs from us as fellow humans is not judgment but love and understanding.

[1]Plato, *Phaedo*, 61.
[2]Thomas Aquinas, *Summa Theologica*, Part II-II, Question 64, Article 5.
[3]John Locke, *The Second Treatise on Civil Government*, Section 6.
[4]Immanuel Kant, *Lectures on Ethics*, trans. Louise Infield (New York: Harper & Row, 1963), Harper Torchbook ed., pp. 153-154.

IV.
REACTIONS
FROM THE
MINISTRY

In her foreword to *Life After Life*, Dr. Elisabeth Kübler-Ross predicted that this type of study would receive criticism from some members of the clergy. To a certain extent this has been true. However, many Christian ministers of various denominations have told me of their enthusiasm and interest in this kind of study and have invited me to speak on the subject to their congregations.

Numerous ministers have told me that they have had parishioners who told them of near-death experiences; they seemed pleased to get the insight of someone whose professional background lies outside the ministry. Quite a few ministers have told me that they feel these experiences confirm things which are said about life after death in *The Bible*. *Guideposts* magazine, which is decidedly Christian in its orientation and outlook, has been publishing accounts such as these for years.

One Methodist minister who had been investigating near-death experiences himself before our paths crossed told me of something that took place after he and I began doing some research together. The following is an excerpt from a dialogue between us about the significance of what we had been doing.

MINISTER: This lady was terminally ill. She had kidney disease. And in talking with her about death before she died, I had affirmed my belief in life after death. I told her that one of the things that had strengthened my faith was the kind of research that had been done by medical doctors in terms of interviewing people who had died and been resuscitated. I had told her about this and it excited her. She brought the thing back up in subsequent visits.

At her funeral, when I delivered the eulogy I mentioned the talks I had with her about this, and how this had tended to affirm her faith. The real thing about this was the way it affected the people in the pews, for me as a clergyman to affirm the fact that I believed that [this lady] was still alive and the fact that a physician friend of mine believes that, too. She had been very close to her husband, and it was like a part of her had died when he died several years before. And I said in that sermon that she had gone to be with him, in some place with Christ. And I wasn't speaking figuratively or symbolically; I meant it. This gave them comfort. . . .

After that funeral an unusual thing happened. People always come up to you after preaching a sermon on Sunday and tell you that you did well, but never after a funeral. It's unheard of. Yet, about ten people afterward came up and complimented me on what I said at that funeral. . . .

One of the things I'm trying to do in preaching is to lead people to love. And if I tell them that at the time of death, Christ comes to people and asks them, "How have you loved?"; that love seems to be a thing Christ points out, not only in *The Bible* back there two thousand years ago but in the now, as people experience death and experience this positive sense of judgment, this affirms faith. This is a tool that I've used several times in preaching to reinforce faith, to lead people to see the importance of faith and love.

DR. MOODY: *You mentioned earlier that like me, you think that a proof of life after death, in the sense of a scientific proof, is not likely to come.*

MINISTER: Well, it we could prove life after death, which would be similar to proving the existence of God, then that would invalidate the system of faith. We cannot prove any of the ultimate things in life. The highest life has to be accepted by faith, and if we were able to short-circuit that and prove that life does exist beyond the grave, people wouldn't have to have any faith in order to believe. Life is a mystery. Life after death is a mystery.

And if we could ever break down the code, then we wouldn't need to operate on faith and this would short-circuit the whole system. So it ultimately must be accepted on faith. But what people who come back from death say does give some affirmation of faith and reinforces it. It affirms my faith, for I am already a man of faith. But if I were not a man of faith, this would not convince me.

That was the opinion of one Methodist minister, but I would not have expected to have every member of the ministry agree. A few ministers have come up with specific objections. One kind of objection has come from some theologically liberal ministers who see the function of the church as essentially an ethical task, having to do with advancing social reform and helping to establish social justice for all. From this theological perspective, they seem to have come to the conclusion that concern with survival of bodily death is old-fashioned. I have heard several such ministers remark that they feel that the concern with life after death is vanishing, or at least that it should be.

In keeping with this viewpoint, an elderly Episcopalian minister recently asked me, in effect, "Shouldn't you think about *this* world, and not the next? Aren't there a lot of problems to be solved *here*?" He went on to say that often in the past, leaders have tried to distract the attention of disadvantaged peoples or other victims of social injustice from their earthly plight by promising that things will be better for them in heaven if they don't get out of line or rock the boat by disobeying the rules. In other words, his antagonism toward the study of near-death phenomena seemed to be based on the concept that doctrines of the afterlife have sometimes represented disguised attempts at social suppression.

To a certain extent I am in agreement with some of the sentiments expressed by these representatives of the ministry. My own feeling is that—yes—there are many real social injustices in this world, and I personally would like, in the course of my own life, to help correct these things. I do feel that the commandment to "love thy neighbor as thyself" is important, and this implies that we should do everything we can to help improve the lot of our fellow man; to help those less fortunate than ourselves.

And yet, there are several points at which my perspective and experience differ from those which these ministers apparently have had. In the light of my own experience, I am surprised to find that some ministers feel that concern over the issue of whether there is personal survival of bodily death is on the wane or is vanishing. My own observation differs sharply. I feel that indeed many people *are* still greatly interested in this issue. Also, I find that I am unable to see how social concern and interest in life after death are mutually exclusive. Surely, one could go on being concerned about the welfare of others even if he were to have full awareness of the fact that there is life after death and an interest in any findings relating to this possibility. In fact, many of the subjects with whom I have talked have expressed intense concern for the welfare of others. They came back from their experiences feeling challenged to live and to get things done for others while here on earth. I personally share these aims. After all, rather than making us indifferent to social injustice, belief in an afterlife may give us an incentive to try to correct it.

Further, I cannot agree that the only—or even a primary—factor in the persistence of doctrines of life after death is to distract people from their unsatisfactory existence. Many persons have told me of their fears of death; they don't like to think that their consciousness may be obliterated at death. Others miss friends and relatives they have lost through death and hope that those persons still live somewhere. These concerns seem far removed from matters of social injustice or class suppression.

In addition, my own approach to these experiences has been shaped by my medical interests. Persons have told me—as a physician—about experiences of theirs which were very significant in their lives and which came about in connection with their contact with medical resuscitation measures. As such, I think that this is a medical issue too. As far as I can, I would like to be able to understand experiences which are very important to my patients and which tend to happen to them in situations in which they are under medical care.

I am not trying to say here that my perspective is any better than that of the ministers I mentioned, only that it is *different*. Thus it could be that their feeling that concern about life after death is fading is a projection of their own limited association with like-minded ministers or with their own socially concerned parishioners. Similarly, however, it could be that my own feeling that concern with this issue is still rampant is a projection of my own limited experience, mainly with many people who did express an interest in this. I don't at all claim to know where the majority of Christian opinion on this issue lies.

The second group of ministers who have voiced criticism of near-death experiences speak from a theological perspective which lies on the conservative side of the spectrum. I am referring to those who say that near-death experiences are directed by satanic forces or evil demons.

I do not have any formal training in the field of theology. My reading in it is largely limited to the works of the great theologians, such as St. Augustine, Thomas Aquinas, and John Calvin, who are also considered great and influential philosophers. But I have asked friends who are ministers and theologians what they think about such charges. The consensus of what they have told me is that a vision is to be counted as valid if, among other things, the effects it has on a person's life are of a certain kind: if it makes him feel closer to God, for example, or it leads him to want to follow religious teachings. As we have seen earlier, the near-death experiences of the persons I have interviewed have led them in precisely these ways. Other ministers have also cited the criterion that such visions must be consistent with what is stated in *The Bible* and have shared with me their feeling that this criterion is satisfied in this case.

For my part, I must confess that it was unsettling to be accused—even if only by implication—of being in league with the devil. My religious belief is very important to me, and one hardly knows how to defend oneself against such an accusation as Satanism. I felt somewhat relieved, however, after talking with a Methodist minister who is of a most conservative and fundamentalist temperament. He assured me that he, too, had been accused by members of a sect which is slightly more conservative than his own of being one of Satan's helpers. I daresay I must content myself with the reflection that in this huge, diverse world there will always be those who impugn one's motivation. I can but hope that, in the respects in which I am in the wrong, someone will come along to help lead me back onto the correct path.

There is a third group of ministers who should be mentioned in connection with this discussion. They have expressed what is not so much criticism as a kind of timidity. They seem to feel inadequate to comment on these experiences because they think of them as lying more in the realm of medicine: a phenomenon which ought to be left to the patient's doctor. They may, for example, discount such experiences by saying that they were merely hallucinations. This is despite the fact that the persons having these experiences relate them to their religious lives and beliefs rather than to their health.

This is yet another manifestation of an old dilemma—the conflict between professions. All professions seem to have certain members who jealously guard their own territory from intrusions by others. Such persons are resentful when an informed layman or a person from another field of study comments on some item relating to their own professional domain. Also, all professions have some members who are reluctant to show interest in or concern for issues that lie outside their personal province or specialty.

It is desirable to be on guard against oversimplification of complex problems, but there are difficulties inherent in this kind of professional exclusivism. This attitude seems to be most stifling intellectually. It is also more likely to shut out any insight which might be contributed to a profession's understanding of its subject matter by outsiders.

In addition, this attitude seems to involve the highly dubious assumption that the present division of labor among professions and fields of study exhausts all reality. I should think that from the point of view of an issue or of a new phenomenon, it must be a horrible fate indeed to be caught in the borderline between the provinces of two human professions.

To relate all of this to the topic at hand, I have met ministers who seem reluctant to talk about anything which appears in any way medical. I have had occasion to meet the ministers of quite a few of my patients, and I was surprised at the apologetic manner some of them displayed when discussing the medical aspects of these cases, especially since they showed a most impressive degree of understanding of the patient's condition and prognosis. So, I have found ministers who will not discuss near-death experiences because they feel that they represent medical phenomena. On the other hand, several physicians have told me that they would not discuss such experiences with their patients because they feel that they are within the realm of the patient's religious life. In short, it appears that to some people this phenomenon is one of those areas lying between two worlds which is predestined to be unpopular.

On the whole I have been pleased that most of the ministers whom I already knew or have met in the course of doing this study have been interested in and have expressed approval of my work. They also realize that I do not draw conclusions, that I am not trying to force my own personal feelings on others and that, being fully aware of my own limitations, I welcome comment and guidance from other perspectives.

V.
HISTORICAL
EXAMPLES

Several years ago, when I was asked whether I knew of any historical examples of the near-death phenomenon, I had to answer in the negative. Since then it has become obvious that there is a wealth of accounts of near-death experiences available in writings from earlier times. I think it would be worthwhile to quote here at length from various sources, drawn from different cultures and ages. What follows is only a fraction of the material I have gathered to date, and what I have already gathered is probably only the tip of the iceberg.

The story of the stoning of the apostle Stephen has been pointed out as a possible near-death experience. In Acts 7:54-58, it is related that just before Stephen was stoned to death by an aroused mob (and apparently before any actual injury took place), he had a vision:

> When they heard these things, they were cut to the heart, and they gnashed on him with their teeth. But he, being full of the Holy Ghost, looked up stedfastly into heaven, and saw the glory of God, and Jesus standing on the right hand of God. And said, Behold, I see the heavens opened, and the Son of man standing on the right hand of God. Then they cried out with a loud voice, and stopped their ears, and ran upon him with one accord, and cast him out of the city, and stoned him: and the witnesses laid down their clothes at a young man's feet, whose name was Saul.

The Venerable Bede was an English monk who lived from 673 to 735 A.D. He completed *A History of the English Church and People* in 731 A.D. Among many wonders, Bede relates a "return from the dead" story which, allowing for differences in cultural idiom, resembles in many respects those heard today.

> About this time, a noteworthy miracle, like those of olden days, occurred in Britain. For, in order to arouse the living from spiritual death, a man already dead returned to bodily life and related many notable things that he had seen, some of which I have thought it valuable to mention here in brief. There was a head of a family living in a place in the country of the Northumbrians known as Cunningham, who led a devout life with all his household. He fell ill and grew steadily worse until the crisis came, and in the early hours of one night he died. But at daybreak he returned to life and suddenly sat up to the great consternation of those weeping around the body, who ran away; only his wife, who loved him more dearly, remained with him, though trembling and fearful. The man reassured her and said: "Do not be frightened; for I have truly risen from the grasp of death, and I am allowed to live

among men again. But henceforward I must not live as I used to, and must adopt a very different way of life." . . . Not long afterward, he abandoned all worldly responsibilities and entered the monastery of Melrose, which is almost completely surrounded by a bend in the river Tweed. . . .

This was the account he used to give of his experience: "A handsome man in a shining robe was my guide, and we walked in silence in what appeared to be a northeasterly direction. As we traveled onward, we came to a very broad and deep valley of infinite length. . . . He soon brought me out of darkness into an atmosphere of clear light, and as he led me forward in bright light, I saw before us a tremendous wall which seemed to be of infinite length and height in all directions. As I could see no gate, window, or entrance in it, I began to wonder why we went up to the wall. But when we reached it, all at once—I know not by what means—we were on top of it. Within lay a very broad and pleasant meadow. . . . Such was the light flooding all this place that it seemed greater than the brightness of daylight or of the sun's rays at noon. . . .

[The guide said,] "You must now return to your body and live among men once more; but, if you will weigh your actions with greater care and study to keep your words and ways virtuous and simple, then when you die you too will win a home among these happy spirits that you see. For when I left you for a while, I did so in order to discover what your future would be.' When he told me this, I was most reluctant to return to my body; for I was entranced by the pleasantness and beauty of the place I could see and the company that I saw there. But I did not dare to question my guide, and meanwhile, I know not how, I suddenly found myself alive among men once more."

This man of God would not discuss these and other things that he had seen with any apathetic or careless-living people, but only with those who were haunted by fear of punishment or gladdened by the hope of eternal joys, and were willing to take his words to heart and grow in holiness.[1]

Features of particular interest in the above narration include the striking way in which the man's life and outlook were changed by his experience, the presence of a spirit who was there to guide him through the transition, and his reluctance to tell this to anyone who would not listen open-mindedly and sympathetically.

Two interesting stories by unknown Irish authors (from the tenth and ninth centuries respectively) appear in an excellent collection of Celtic literature, *A Celtic Miscellany*, translated by Kenneth H. Jackson.

The Little Boys Who Went to Heaven

. . . Donnán, son of Liath, one of Senán's disciples, went to gather dulse on the shore, with two little boys who were studying along with him. The sea carried off his boat from him, so that he had no boat to fetch the boys, and there was no other boat on the island to rescue the boys. So the boys were drowned on a rock; but on the next day their bodies were carried so that they lay on the beach of the island. The parents came then and stood on the beach, and asked that their sons should be given them alive. Senán said to Donnán, "Tell the boys to arise and speak with me." Donnán said to the boys, "You may arise to talk with your parents, for Senán tells you to do so." They arose at once at Senán's command, and said to their parents, "You have done wrong to us, bringing us away from the land to which we came." "How could you prefer," said their mother to them, "to stay in that land rather than to come to us?" "Mother," they said, "though you should give us power over the whole world, and all its enjoyment and delight, we should think it no different from being in prison, compared with being in the life and in the world to which we came. Do not delay us, for it is time for us to go back again to the land from which we have come; and God shall bring it about for our sake that you shall not mourn after us." So their parents gave them their consent, and they went together with Senán to his oratory; and the sacrament was given them, and they went to heaven, and their bodies were buried in front of the oratory where Senán lived. And these were the first dead who were buried in Scattery Island.

A Ghost Story

There were two students who were studying together, so that they were foster-brothers since they were small children. This was their talk, in their little hut: "It is a sad journey on which our dear ones and our friends go from us, that they never come back again with news for us of the land to which they go. Let us make a plan, that whoever of us dies first should come with news to the other." "Let it be done, truly." They undertook that whoever of them should die first should come before the end of a month with news to the other.

Not long after this, then, one of the two died. He was buried by the other, and he sang his requiem. He was expecting him until the end of a month, but the other did not come; and he was abusing him and abusing the Trinity, so that the soul begged the Trinity to let it go to talk with him. Now, the latter was making prostrations in his hut, and there was a little lintel above his head; his head struck against the lintel so that he fell lifeless. His soul saw the body lying before it, but it thought it was still in its body. It was looking at it. "But this is bad," it said, "to bring me a dead body. It is the brotherhood of the church, truly," it said, "who have brought it." At that it bounded out of the house. One of the clergy was ringing the bell. "It is not right, priest," it said, "to bring the dead body to me." The priest did not answer. It betook itself to everyone. They did not hear. It was greatly distressed. It betook itself out of the church to the reapers. "Here I am," it said. They did not hear. Fury seized it. It went to its church again. They had gone to take tithes to him, and his body was seen in the house, and it was brought to the graveyard.

When the soul went into the church, it saw its friend before it. "Well now," it said, "you have been a long time coming; yours was a bad promise." "Do not reproach me," said the other, "I have come many a time, and would be beside your pillow pleading with you, and you did not hear; for the dense heavy body does not hear the light ethereal tenuous soul." "I hear you now," it said. "No," said the other, "it is your soul only that is here. It is from your own body that you are escaping. For you have begged me to meet you, and that has come about, then. Woe is him who does wrong! Happy is he who does right! Go to find your body before it is put into the grave." "I will never go into it again, for horror and fear of it!" "You shall go; you shall be alive for a year. Recite the *Beati* every day for my soul, for the *Beati* is the strongest ladder and chain and collar to bring a man's soul out of hell."

It said farewell to the other, and went to its body, and as it went into it it gave a shriek, and came back to life; and went to heaven at the end of a year. So the *Beati* is the best prayer there is.[2]

In these two accounts there are features found in many contemporary experiences. In both of these stories we have the now familiar "reluctance to return." In the second there is the feeling that the spirit has departed the body. The student views his body, which he fails at first to recognize as his own (a remark which several persons have made to me in describing their experiences). He notices the "one-way mirror" effect; that is although he is able to hear and see others, he is apparently invisible and inaudible to them. Also, he is greeted by his departed friend.

An interesting account from another culture is given in a book by Sir Edward Burnett Tylor, a nineteenth-century English anthropologist. In *Primitive Culture*, he quotes the following Polynesian story.

This story . . . was told to Mr. Shortland by a servant of his named Te Wharewera. An aunt of this man died in a solitary hut near the banks of Lake Rotorua. Being a lady of rank she was left in her hut, the door and windows were made fast, and the dwelling was abandoned, as her death had made it tapu. But a day or two after, Te Wharewera with some others paddling in a canoe near the place at early morning saw a figure on the shore beckoning to them. It was the aunt come to life again, but weak and cold and famished. When sufficiently restored by their timely help, she told her story. Leaving her body, her spirit had taken the flight toward the North Cape, and arrived at the entrance of Reigna. There, holding on by the stem of the creeping akeake plant, she descended the precipice, and found herself on the sandy beach of a river. Looking around, she espied in the distance an enormous bird, taller than a man, coming toward her with rapid strides. This terrible object so frightened her that her first thought was to try to return up the steep cliff; but seeing an old man paddling a small canoe toward her she ran to meet him, and so escaped the bird. When she had been safely ferried across she asked the old Charon, mentioning the name of her family, where the spirits of her kindred dwelt. Following the path the old man pointed out, she was surprised to find it just such a path as she had been used to on earth; the aspect of the country, the trees, shrubs, and plants were all familiar to her. She reached the village and among the crowd assembled there she found her father and many near relations; they saluted her, and welcomed her with the wailing chant which Maoris always address to people met after long absence. But when her father had asked about his living relatives, and especially about her own child, he told her she must go back to earth, for no one was left to take care of his grandchild. By his orders she refused to touch the food that the dead people offered her, and in spite of their efforts to detain her, her father got her safely into the canoe, crossed with her, and parting gave her from under his cloak two enormous sweet potatoes to plant at home for his grandchild's especial eating. But as she began to climb the precipice again, two pursuing infant spirits pulled her back, and she only escaped by flinging the roots at them, which they stopped to eat, while she scaled the rock by help of the akeake stem, till she reached the earth and flew back to where she had left her body. On returning to life she found herself in darkness, and what had passed seemed as a dream, till she perceived that she was deserted and the door fast, and concluded that she had really died and come to life again. When morning dawned, a faint light entered by the crevices of the shut-up house, and she saw on the floor near her a calabash partly full of red ocher mixed with water; this she eagerly drained to the dregs, and then feeling a little stronger, succeeded in opening the door and crawling down to the beach, where her friends soon after found her. Those who listened to her tale firmly believed the reality of her adventures, but it was much regretted that she had not brought back at least one of the huge sweet potatoes as evidence of her visit to the land of spirits.[3]

I have been unable to find Edward Shortland's *Traditions and Superstitions of the New Zealanders*, from which Tylor summarizes. However, even allowing for cultural variation in expression and symbolization and for the garbling which probably took place as the story was passed from person to person, one recognizes several of the common elements of near-death experiences which have been discussed. The woman who "died" left her body, crossed a river, was met by departed relatives, and was told that she had to go back to care for her son.

The English writer Thomas De Quincey (1785-1859) was familiar with near-death experiences. In *Confessions of an English Opium Eater* he describes his own problems with opium addiction, a habit which was quite widespread in his day, when opium was freely available and easily and legally purchased. He describes how sometimes scenes from his past would come back to him, and this reminds him of a story related to him by a female relative, widely believed by scholars to have been his mother.

In the first (1821) edition of his book, he writes:

> I was once told by a near relative of mine, that having in her childhood fallen into a river, and being on the very verge of death but for the critical assistance which reached her, she saw in a moment her whole life, in its minutest incidents, arrayed before her simultaneously as in a mirror; and she had a faculty developed as suddenly for comprehending the whole and every part.[4]

In a sequel, *Suspiria De Profundis*, De Quincey elaborates further on this incident and remarks on the skeptical response his retelling of it apparently elicited in some readers.

> The lady is still living, though now of unusually great age; and I may mention that among her faults never was numbered any levity of principle, or carelessness of the most scrupulous veracity; but, on the contary, such faults as arise from austerity, too harsh, perhaps, and gloomy, indulgent neither to others nor herself. And, at the time of relating this incident, when already very old, she had become religious to asceticism. According to my present belief, she had completed her ninth year, when, playing by the side of a solitary brook, she fell into one of its deepest pools. Eventually, but after what lapse of time nobody ever knew, she was saved from death by a farmer, who, riding in some distant lane, had seen her rise to the surface; but not until she had descended within the abyss of death, and looked into its secrets, as far, perhaps, as ever human eye *can* have looked that had permission to return. At a certain stage of this descent, a blow seemed to strike her; phosphoric radiance sprang forth from her

eyeballs; and immediately a mighty theater expanded within her brain. In a moment, in the twinkling of an eye, every act, every design of her past life, lived again, arraying themselves not as a succession, but as parts of a coexistence. Such a light fell upon the whole path of her life backward into the shades of infancy as the light, perhaps, which wrapt the destined apostle [Paul] on his road to Damascus. Yet that light blinded for a season; but hers poured celestial vision upon the brain, so that her consciousness became omnipresent at one moment to every feature in the infinite review.

This anecdote was treated skeptically at the time by some critics. But, besides that it has since been confirmed by other experience essentially the same, reported by other parties in the same circumstances, who had never heard of each other, the true point for astonishment is not the *simultaneity* of arrangement under which the past events of life, though in fact successive, had formed their dread line of revelation. This was but a secondary phenomenon; the deeper lay in the resurrection itself, and the possibility of resurrection, for what had so long slept in the dust. A pall, deep as oblivion, had been thrown by life over every trace of these experiences; and yet suddenly, at a silent command, at the signal of a blazing rocket sent up from the brain, the pall draws up, and the whole depths of the theater are exposed.[5]

With respect to more recent times, it is noteworthy that members of the Church of Jesus Christ of Latter-Day Saints (the Mormons) have been aware of accounts of near-death experiences for many years and circulate these stories among themselves. Also interesting is the fact that the renowned psychiatrist Carl Gustav Jung had a near-death experience, he describes it in the section entiled "Visions" in the book *Memories, Dreams, and Reflections.*

Oscar Lewis, a contemporary anthropologist, wrote a fascinating work, *The Children of Sánchez*, based on his studies of life in a Mexican family. One of the members of the family related a near-death experience to him.

There are similar descriptions in literature. To give only two, Ernest Hemingway, in *A Farewell to Arms*, has the narrator describe how he had the sensation of being out of his body during a close call with death. (This is interesting in that some say that this novel is largely autobiographical.) And Count Leo Tolstoy, in *The Death of Ivan Ilyich*, describes the death scene of Ivan Ilyich in terms of being in a dark, cavelike space, of having a flashback of his past life, and at last, of entering into a brilliant light.

Again, the above are only a few of the many accounts available. Far from being a new phenomenon, near-death experiences have been with us for a long, long time.

[1]Bede, *A History of the English Church and People*, trans. Leo Sherley-Price (Harmondsworth, England: Penguin Books, 1968), pp. 289-293.

[2]Kenneth Hurlstone Jackson, *A Celtic Miscellany* (Harmondsworth, England: Penguin Books, 1971), pp. 285-287.

[3]Edward Burnett Tylor, *Primitive Culture*, Vol. II (New York: Henry Holt and Co., 1874), pp. 50-52.

[4]Thomas De Quincey, *Confessions of an English Opium Eater with Its Sequels Suspiria De Profundis and The English Mail-Coach*, ed. Malcolm Elwin (London: Macdonald & Co., 1956), pp. 420-421.

[5]Ibid., pp. 511-512.

VI.
MORE QUESTIONS

Since the publication of *Life After Life*, I have received many questions from readers of the book, from medical and academic colleagues, and from other interested individuals. I feel that many of these questions are of general interest, and so I shall answer them through the forum of this second book.

Won't the broad public discussion of the details of this phenomenon interfere with the accuracy of future research in this area?

This is a difficult issue, of course. It does raise the specter not only of subsequent experiences being shaped by reading accounts of earlier ones, but also the possibility that unscrupulous persons may falsely allege that they have been through such experiences in order to attract attention and publicity, or to achieve some other dubious advantage. However, even though my study and those of Dr. Kübler-Ross and other investigators in this field may complicate the problem of separating the wheat from the chaff, I still think that if the phenomenon is ever to be studied scientifically it must first be brought to the foreground.

The alternative is to keep it a professional secret and this, too, is full of objections and perplexities. For years the question very frequently asked me has been, "If such things are so commonly experienced, why haven't they been more widely publicized?" Now, it's beginning to appear that we might go through a time in which the question will be, "Since such things are so widely publicized, is it any wonder that they're so commonly experienced?"

Why don't you use the names of the people you have interviewed? Wouldn't this make your work more credible?

It will continue to be my policy not to use names. There are several reasons for this. People have come to me under the assumption that I would not be using their names. I want to continue this practice so that I can continue collecting accounts which people might not give me if they felt that they would be identified. It might well make more tantalizing reading if I were to print a picture of a person and give out his name and address, as one might do in a newspaper article. However, this would not make my study more credible from a scientific point of view.

What will make this more real, ultimately, is for others to find the same things I have in different cases. In my book I draw no conclusions: I only make a prediction that others who pursue this matter sympathetically and diligently will be able to find examples of near-death experiences which demonstrate all of the various elements and stages of the experiences about which I have written.

Isn't this whole concept of life after death just so much wishful thinking?

Some might argue that since all, or at least, most of us, would wish to live after death, any evidence which is presented to that effect should be regarded suspiciously. Such arguments abound in many quarters, but I might point out that this can work the other way too. The fact that there is something that most of us desire does not imply that it does not occur.

William James put it very well when he said in effect, that with respect to religious matters which are not susceptible to empirical proof or disproof, it did not appear any more rational to disbelieve them out of fear of being wrong than it was to believe out of hope of being right.

Isn't interest in near-death experiences just a "fad"?

I doubt it. Concern with the nature and meaning of death has endured throughout the history of Western thought. Almost all of the great philosophers have dealt with this issue, and it can be seen almost as the central theme of the writings and systems of many of them.

Secondly, the rapid progress in resuscitation technology almost guarantees that we will be dealing with this phenomenon increasingly in the future.

Finally, many doctors must have heard from terminally ill patients the anguished plea, "Can't anyone tell me what it is like to die?" Regardless of whether one conceives of near-death experiences as intimations of immortality or merely as the result of terminal physiological events, I think that it is a gain that we are beginning to be able to shed a little more light on that question.

Were the people with whom you have talked interested in the occult either prior to or after their experience?

I have talked with more than three hundred people now who have had near-death experiences. In a group that size it is not surprising that one would find a few who did have some sort of interest in such matters as reincarnation, communication with spirits through mediums, astrology, and other occult phenomena. However, it is quite interesting to me that out of my group of subjects, only six or seven expressed any sort of interest in this area, either before or after their experience. Almost none of these people have reported having more than one uncanny or unusual experience in the course of their lives.

By and large, the people with whom I have talked are not people who frequently have unusual experiences, or who have any more than the average interest in occult matters.

Have you ever interviewed any atheists who had these experiences?

Everyone with whom I have talked came from within the Judeo-Christian tradition.

In that context the word "atheist" is, at least in part, a "judgmental" term that entails a certain interpretation of personality, feelings, and belief. "Atheism" may be, in some cases, just verbal behavior masking personal feelings that may be very different, perhaps even deeply religious.

I feel that it would be almost impossible to determine the degree of prior religious belief in these cases, since everyone in our society is at least exposed to religious concepts. In view of this, the question would always arise for any person to what degree—even unconsciously—he already holds to religious concepts.

The persons I interviewed who stated that they had no particular religious beliefs prior to their near-death experiences, did state that after having this experience they now accept as true the religious doctrines of a hereafter.

What was the age range of the persons whom you interviewed?

I have talked with several adults who were telling me of experiences which took place when they were children. The youngest age in these reports was three years. However, I have talked to only one child who told me of his experience and this was quite by coincidence. He just happened to tell it to me in a pediatrics clinic when I was helping to treat him.

The oldest person with whom I have talked was approximately seventy-five at the time of his experience. Of course, the thoughts which go through a child's mind at this time of crisis are different from those which occur to an adult, and he may express them differently.

Isn't the effect of all this to glorify death?

No, absolutely not. I think that we all recognize the bad aspects of death. Death is bad in its aspects of separation from loved ones and in the suffering from illness or injury that can take place before it. It is also bad in that people may die prematurely before having a chance to complete things which they want to accomplish in life.

I "died" and was resuscitated. Yet, I remember nothing at all about it. What's wrong with me?

Several people have expressed this kind of worry to me, and in response I want to take the opportunity to make several remarks. As I emphasized in *Life After Life*, not everyone who survives a clinical "death" remembers anything whatsoever about it. I have talked with many people who remember nothing about it.

I can't detect *any* difference between those who do and those who don't have such experiences during their "death" in their religious background or personality, in the circumstances or cause of "death," or in any other factor.

One wonders whether a certain percentage of the people who remember nothing might not be suppressing this material, that is, whether there might not have been an experience at the time which the subconscious mind, for one reason or another, forced the conscious mind to "forget."

I want very much for others to avoid taking my list of common elements as being a fixed, exhaustive model of what a near-death experience *must* be like. There is an enormously wide spectrum of experiences, with some people having only one or two of the elements, and others most of them. I anticipate that the list I have developed will be added to, modified, and reformulated. Such a list is only intended as a rough-and-ready theoretical model, and one ought to avoid any temptation of making it into a fixed ideal.

You say that not everyone who goes through an apparent clinical death has any experience. What percentage do?

The kind of study which I have done does not give me a basis on which to make such a judgment. In the first place, my sample of cases is obviously weighted toward those who did have an experience. Due to the nature of what I am doing, those who have experiences would be more likely to tell me about them than would those who went through a clinical death and remember nothing.

A similar question has been often posed about the individual elements of near-death experiences. People ask, for instance, what percentage of the people report going through the tunnel or seeing the "being of light", etc. I have not attempted to calculate what percentage of people report each element. Firstly, one cannot be sure that because a person didn't include a given element in recounting his experience, the element wasn't present. He may have forgotten it, or had some reason for omitting it. Secondly, I haven't bothered to count because such an exercise would yield only pseudoscientific number magic.

It would have been a simple matter to have illustrated both my books with graphs and charts showing such figures and percentages. However, since my sample of cases is not random and was not collected under controlled circumstances, such graphs and charts would only represent self-deception and have no scientific validity.

The only way questions such as these could be answered

satisfactorily from a scientific point of view would be to do prospective studies of the kind which I will try to describe more fully in the Appendix. For example, the next 250 cases of successful cardiopulmonary resuscitation attempts in a given hospital might be investigated under given controlled conditions to test given experimental hypotheses.

In spite of the lack of statistical evidence, I feel that near-death experiences of the type I have described are common among persons who have been resuscitated. I predict that any investigator who enters into this type of study sympathetically and diligently will find that there is ample case material.

Have you ever interviewed a person about a near-death experience by placing him under hypnosis?

I once thought that, given willing subjects, this could conceivably be a fruitful avenue to follow. In fact, I was in the preliminary stages of planning an investigation of this sort with the cooperation of a skilled and experienced medical hypnotist. However, it occurred to us that, theoretically, attempting to take a person back in time to the moment of his clinical death could be dangerous. The subconscious mind takes hypnotic suggestions very literally. In addition, hypnotic suggestions can have surprising and odd effects on the body and its function. For example, it is said that a blister may be raised on the skin of a hypnotized person merely by suggesting that a very hot object has been touched to his skin.

Considering this, we thought that in obeying the suggestion to go back mentally to the moment of a clinical "death," a person could literally go through the physiological events of death again. So we never tried our experiment of this kind in which the patient actually did go into cardiac failure and had to be brought out of it! Needless to say, such experiments are to be frowned upon.

Should one tell terminally ill patients about these experiences?

Several physicians have asked me this. I have never resolved it satisfactorily in my own mind, since there are so many variables. On the negative side, one could argue that this knowledge might disturb people who have a fixed theology which holds that very different kinds of events unfold after death—or that no events at all transpire. In this case, one can well argue that one should not tell them because it may disturb them, especially if they have already made their peace with death in their own fashion.

On the other hand, I have heard it argued that there are some people who should be told. If these reports are not true and there is no life after death, no harm was done. But if the reports are true, people might be better prepared for what lies ahead for them. *The Tibetan Book of the Dead* was apparently written for this purpose. One idea behind it was that it could be read to those who were dying (and, for a while after they died) so that they would be less confused about the states through which they were going.

I think the ultimate answer to this question depends on the persons involved. Physicians would have to depend upon their clinical judgment, their knowledge of what kind of person their patient is, and the particular doctor-patient relationship that exists.

At any rate, this question may soon be academic, since it appears that the fact that such experiences occur is becoming increasingly known. In this regard, I might mention a proposal made by a pediatrician who has dealt with many terminally ill patients. She suggests that people who have had near-death experiences share them with terminally ill persons who express interest in hearing about them.

How should one respond when an acquaintance (or a patient) reports such an experience without being asked?

This question has presented itself to me in a very personal way. Curiously enough, I have never interviewed a patient whom I helped to resuscitate. However, during the course of my medical education, I did have two patients who spontaneously described near-death experiences to me. In both cases, the experiences had taken place some months earlier and in neither case had I asked the patient anything connected with this topic. They simply recounted their experiences in the course of the usual kind of conversation that goes on between doctor and patient.

I found both these events striking in that they provided further confirmation of my belief that one reason that physicians have not heretofore noticed this phenomenon very much is that they simply don't hear it when patients tell them about such occurrences.

One of the patients was an elderly man with a skin problem; the other was a retarded twelve-year-old boy who had a congenital endocrine disease. Neither knew that I had been doing a study of near-death experiences. I was so taken aback at the unexpectedness of these disclosures that what I ended up doing, in effect, was nothing. In each instance, I made some innocuous remark like "That's interesting," and didn't press the matter further. I suppose I felt at the time that these patients were there for help with a specific medical problem and that the clinic was not the appropriate place to pursue this kind of discussion. I gave no indication to either patient that I had ever heard of such an experience before.

As I look back, I have a sense of guilt that I did not share my knowledge of these experiences with these two people. Perhaps hearing that these experiences had also happened to others would have been the most important kind of support that I could have given them.

My present feeling is that, again depending on the particular relationship involved, one might respond by saying something along the following lines: "Such experiences occur, and many have reported them. Though from a scientific and medical standpoint, one cannot make a specific statement about what they represent, the experience must have meant a great deal to you. Ultimately it will be for you to understand it and integrate it into your own life. You may find help in gaining understanding by reading great religious writings and by discussions with other people who have had these experiences or who have investigated or thought about them."

Should the fact that one knows about such experiences affect one's care of a dying patient?

This is a very complex issue. One thing that occurs to me is that one should be very careful about what is said at resuscitation attempts, even when it seems obvious that the patient is lost. Many physicians have been surprised to hear their remarks quoted to them by the patient after a successful resuscitation attempt. I know of one physician who in his practice deals with many terminally ill patients. He knew of many experiences of the kind I have written about even before he read of my research. He has developed the practice of staying with his patients for a while after they have died and taking care of them by talking to them. Interestingly, he does this even though he personally believes near-death experiences represent nothing more than physiological processes that continue in the brain for a while even after the heart has stopped beating.

What implications do studies of near-death phenomena have for the ethical issues surrounding maintaining life artificially, even after brain function has been unalterably impaired?

The implications of these studies may be very important for cases in which life is sustained artifically. However, the state of research in this area is so elementary right now that no conclusions whatsoever can be drawn. Even if the reality of near-death phenomena were to come to be taken as established scientific fact, and not a matter lying in the realm of anecdote and speculation, these ethical dilemmas would still exist.

With respect to the specific question concerning so-called "mercy killing," however, my opinion is more dogmatic. I am opposed to it on ethical grounds and would not recommend it under any conditions.

I am a member of an emergency medical team and am frequently involved in trying to revive patients with essentially no vital signs. It is troubling to learn from these patients, as one occasionally does, that they resented the efforts to bring them back because they were having one of these experiences. How is one to deal emotionally with this?

I've heard stories, too, both from patients and from doctors, about happenings like this. However, in my experience, this has been a temporary response. They might resent the resuscitation measures at the time, but from the perspective of a few hours, days, or weeks, their attitude changes. They, by and large, become very grateful that they have been given "a second chance."

Some of your subjects have said that they came to believe that the ability to love others and the accumulation of knowledge were the two most important goals to seek in life. Could you elaborate more fully on this? What kind of love? What kind of knowledge?

Both "love" and "knowledge" are English words which are highly ambiguous. The Greek words *philos, eros,* and *agapé,* despite the fact that they express very different concepts, could all three be translated into English as "love"! I gather from the tone of the persons who report these experiences that the kind of love they have in mind is probably closest to the concept of *agapé.* It can be characterized, generally, as an overflowing, spontaneous, unmotivated kind of love which is given to others regardless of of their faults.

Similarly, the Greek words *epistémé* and *techné,* again with very different meanings, would both be translated as "knowledge." *Techné,* as is implied in the use of its English cognates "technology" and "technique," has partly to do with what one might call the application of knowledge. *Epistémé* deals more with factual and theoretical kinds of knowledge. My impression from listening to stories of near-death experiences is that the kind of knowledge people mean has more to do with theoretical and factual kinds of things. No one seems to have come back, for instance, with the impassioned desire to learn how to ride a bicycle, despite the fact that one can talk in English of "knowing" how to ride a bicycle.

Recently I have been asking people who have had near-death experiences to explain as well as they could what kind of love or knowledge they felt was important. One subject was a man in his forties who had been involved in a severe automobile accident. He was taken to a hospital where his condition was declared hopeless, but he was resuscitated. In an interview which took place about a month later, he said the following:

> [About love] Now, he asked me about love. How far had I learned to love? What he was asking was obvious to me then, but it is so hard to explain now. He wanted me to understand that it was the kind of love that has nothing to do with downgrading people. Could I love people, even when I knew them really well, even their faults, was what he was asking.

> [About knowledge] The knowledge that I had gained: that was mentioned, too . . . What kind of knowledge? Well, it's hard to say, you know. But it was knowledge of basic things, causes of things, the basic universal principles . . . of things that hold the universe together . . . I was told that that would be important over there, too . . .

The following excerpts are from an interview with a housewife in her late thirties who had developed complications after surgery and suffered a heart arrest.

> [About love] He showed me all that I had done, and then he asked me if I was satisfied with my life . . . He was interested in love. Love was it. And he meant the kind of love that makes me want to know if my neighbor is fed and clothed and makes me want to help him, if he is not.

> [About knowledge] The kind of knowledge meant was

deeper knowledge, sort of as it related to the soul . . .
wisdom, I would say.

It is quite clear that love was the goal that was most emphasized in the reviews of their lives which these two people
witnessed. When knowledge was mentioned by the "being of
light," it was often done in a casual and almost offhand way. He
implied that learning was not something that stopped at
people's death but would continue even when they came over
there permanently.

Bear in mind that this discussion is complicated by the fact
that people say that in order to express the full impact of the
experience, they would need language far beyond their
capabilities. The words they are able to use are inadequate.
Indeed, the ultimate realities are ineffable.

There is another Greek word, *sophia*, which also has to do
with knowledge. *Sophia* would be translated into English as
"wisdom," and it is significant that precisely this term comes
up in one of the accounts quoted above. *Sophia* and "wisdom"
alike have—if one may put it this way—an ethical dimension
as well as a factual one. The wise man, presumably, would not
only possess knowledge but would be able to apply it in a
morally correct way. So the account quoted implies a moral
aspect to the accumulation of knowledge.

*Can't people have similar or the same experiences as you have
described without "dying" or even coming near death?*

Yes, apparently so. Many people have told me of out-of-
body experiences which took place spontaneously. The persons involved were not "dead" or even ill or in jeopardy.
Further, in most cases these experiences were not being
sought out in any way. They came as complete surprises.

Near-death experiences are also similar in many respects to
mystical and religious visions described by great seers in the
past. Many more examples of similarities could, no doubt, be
cited. However, I have not sought out such accounts or followed up the ones that were reported to me. This is not

because I am not interested in them. It is just that I have found more than enough material to keep me busy concentrating on those in which a near-death encounter does take place.

If I were asked how I account for these similarities and allowed to be wildly speculative, I could think of any number of possible explanations. For example, let us take as a hypothesis that there is a direct continuation of life after physical death. If this is so, there must be some mechanism— bodily or spiritual or maybe both—that releases the psyche, the soul (or whatever one wants to call it), from the body upon physical death. Now, we don't assume that our bodily mechanisms work perfectly every time. The organs of our body sometimes malfunction and our reason, perception, or thinking may sometimes lead us astray. Analogously, we have no reason to assume that this hypothetical mechanism for releasing the soul from the body always would work perfectly. Might it not be that different kinds of situations—stresses, etc.—could sometimes work to set off this mechanism prematurely? If all this were true, then it could explain the similarity between near-death experiences and other kinds, such as out-of-body experiences. It could also explain the fact that the phenomena reported by those who find themselves in life-threatening situations without even being injured can be identical with the experiences of those who are revived after an apparent clinical "death."

You have just said that mystical visions are similar in many respects to near-death experiences. What are the points of similarity?

Many people these days seem to regard "mysticism" as synonymous with "Oriental mysticism." However, there is a long history of mystical visions in the Western tradition. St. Augustine, St. Francis of Assisi, Teresa of Avila, Meister Eckhardt, and Joan of Arc all could be called mystics.

In his famous study *The Varieties of Religious Experience*, William James gives the following list of the characteristics of mystical visions.

1. *Ineffability*—The handiest of the marks by which I classify a state of mind as mystical is negative. The subject of it immediately says that it defies expression, that no adequate report of its contents can be given in words. . . .

2. *Noetic quality*—Mystical states seem to those who experience them to be also states of knowledge. They are states of insight into depths of truth unplumbed by the discursive intellect. . . .

These two characters will entitle any state to be called mystical, in the sense in which I use the word. Two other qualities are less sharply marked, but are usually found. These are:

3. *Transiency*—Mystical states cannot be sustained for long. Except in rare instances, half an hour, or at most an hour or two, seems to be the limit beyond which they fade into the light of common day. . . .

4. *Passivity*—Although the oncoming of mystical states may be facilitated by preliminary voluntary operations, as by fixing the attention, or going through certain bodily performances, or in other ways which manuals of mysticism prescribe; yet when the characteristic sort of consciousness once has set in, the mystic feels as if his own will were in abeyance, and indeed sometimes as if he were grasped and held by a superior power. This latter peculiarity connects mystical states with certain definite phenomena of secondary or alternative personality, such as prophetic speech, automatic writing, or the mediumistic trance. When these latter conditions are well pronounced, however, there may be no recollection whatever of the phenomenon, and it may have no significance for the subject's usual inner life, to which, as it were, it makes a mere interruption. Mystical states, strictly so called, are never merely interruptive. Some memory of their content always remains, and a profound sense of their importance. They modify the inner life of the subject between the times of their recurrence. Sharp divi-

sions in this region are, however, difficult to make, and we find all sorts of gradations and mixtures.[1]

Others have pointed out additional characteristics. Two examples are the occurrence of an altered sense of time and space and an integrating effect—in many cases—of the vision on the personality and subsequent life of the individual.

All of the criteria above obviously apply in one way or another to the case of near-death experiences. However, there are other very common features of near-death experiences which have not figured prominently as aspects of the experiences of the great mystics of history. The panoramic review of one's life is an example.

Do people say that their sense of time is changed during these experiences?

It is very commonly reported that during near-death experiences, time is altered. This comes much to the fore in remarks like that of one woman who during an apparent clinical "death" seemed to find herself in paradisiacal surroundings. When I asked how long this seemed to take she said, "You could say a minute or you could say ten thousand years. It doesn't make any difference."

Again, a man who was trapped in an explosion and fire seemed to float above his body and to see others as they ran to rescue him. He says that at this point his physical surroundings seemed to disappear entirely and a review of his entire life came before him, while he "discussed" it in the presence of "Christ." When asked how long the review seemed to take, he remarked that if he were forced to put it in temporal terms he would have to say that it took an hour at the very least. Yet, when he was told he must return and the review disappeared, he again saw his physical surroundings. The persons he saw coming to rescue him seemed frozen in stop motion, in the same positions they had been just as the review started. When he seemed to be returning to his body, the action speeded up again.

These examples and many more illustrate how, during near-death experiences, to use the words of yet another person, "Time there isn't like time here" One might point to this as yet another feature in which near-death experiences resemble mystical visions.

Do people who are out of their bodies during near-death experiences feel pain?

Many people have told me that while they felt they were out of their bodies they sensed no pain whatsoever, even though they may have been in great pain just prior to this. Some have reported with amazement that even though they could see their physicians or other medical personnel pounding on their chests, sticking IV needles into their arms, etc., while in the out-of-body state, they felt no pain at all from these activities. On the other hand, people have reported that as soon as they re-entered their bodies, they were immediately seized again by pain.

You have mentioned cases of near-death experiences of extreme duration. How is it possible that these people were revived without serious brain damage?

Several facts could be brought up here. First of all, during resuscitation procedures, the brain *is* being perfused with blood and with oxygen and nourishment it carries. This is the point of cardiac massage: to keep the blood flowing even though the heart is not beating by itself.

Secondly, conditions such as variations in temperature can affect the rate at which the brain may be damaged. The brain of a person who had a temperature of 105° just prior to death would deteriorate more rapidly than that of a person whose body temperature had been lowered. Indeed, during operations such as open heart surgery the heart has been stopped for long periods without the person's brain being perfused, without attendant brain damage. This was made possible by the use of hypothermic techniques; the brain temperature was artificially lowered.

So, although many have heard that after five minutes without oxygen resuscitation without brain damage is impossible, this is only a simplified rule. All sorts of other factors must be taken into account considering the complex circumstances of a resuscitation attempt. Indeed, severe brain damage is not usual among patients who are revived after a cardiac arrest.

You have said that near-death experiences have become much more common in recent decades due to developments in resuscitation techniques. Was there any kind of resuscitation before the advent of modern medicine?

Resuscitation itself, in one form or another, is a very ancient technique. Phoenician medical tablets thousands of years old have described techniques of resuscitation by mouth-to-mouth respiration. Also, we find in *The Bible*, in II Kings 4:18-37, the following rather remarkable narrative.

And when the child was grown, it fell on a day, that he went out to his father to the reapers, and he said unto his father, My head, my head. And he said to a lad, carry him to his mother. And when he had taken him, and brought him to his mother, he sat on her knees till noon, and then died. And she went up, and laid him on the bed of the man of God, and shut the door upon him, and went out. . . . Then she saddled an ass, and said to her servant, Drive, and go forward . . . So she went and came unto the man of God . . . And he arose, and followed her. . . . And when Elisha was come into the house, behold the child was dead, and laid upon his bed. He went in therefore, and shut the door upon them twain, and prayed unto the Lord. And he went up, and lay upon the child, and put his mouth upon his mouth, and his eyes upon his eyes, and his hands upon his hands; and he stretched himself upon the child; and the flesh of the child waxed warm. Then he returned, and walked in the house to and fro; and went up, and stretched himself upon him: and the child sneezed seven times, and the child opened his eyes. . . . And when she [the mother] was come in unto him, he said, Take up thy son. Then she went in, and fell at his feet, and bowed herself to the ground, and took up her son, and went out.

A similar but somewhat less detailed story is found in I Kings 17. An interesting detail in the passage from II Kings just quoted is that the boy sneezed upon being revived. It is a folk belief of many peoples that a sneeze is a sign that the soul has re-entered the body after having briefly left it. This otherwise puzzling little detail is probably a reflection of this belief.

Among techniques of resuscitation known and used in very early times was applying heat to the abdomen of the victim. Another was flagellation; pain was inflicted on the unconscious person by flogging him with nettles in hopes of reviving him. No doubt other methods were used as well, but a significant advance, which may seem more "scientific" to contemporary minds, was achieved by the Renaissance physician Paracelsus, a German who lived from 1493 until 1541. He introduced the procedure of resuscitating the apparently dead or near-dead by forcing air into their lungs with the common bellows—which was, then as now, used by the fireplace. Vesalius (1514-1564), another outstanding physician of that period, also used the bellows for resuscitation and did experiments with artificial respiration. The bellows method was subsequently used in Europe for several centuries. Many other techniques, including rolling a nearly drowned person over a barrel, and laying a person over the back of a horse and trotting the horse, have been used over the centuries in different societies. The method of restarting the heart by injections of adrenalin (epinephrine) was developed as long ago as 1905 by Winter.

Techniques of resuscitation have a long history, not only in Western and Judeo-Christian societies but also in what we call "primitive" cultures. For example, some Indians of North

America used a method in which smoke contained in a syringe-like instrument was forced into the victim's rectum. Despite the fact that this technique sounds implausible, it is alleged that it was used successfully in the American colonies for some time and was introduced into Great Britain in the latter part of the eighteenth century.

Since close calls with death are common in every society from the most primitive to the most highly developed, I have wondered whether the occurrence of near-death experiences might not be part of the explanation for a certain very ancient and widespread concept of disease. All over the world, and far back into history, many have believed that in certain instances sickness was caused by the soul's leaving the body. Where such beliefs are accepted, treatment is directed toward persuading or forcing the patient to get back into his body. One can point to other such folk beliefs—for example, that of the inhabitants of central Celebes, an island in eastern Indonesia, that the soul may leave the body when a person is suddenly and unexpectedly frightened—and wonder whether these beliefs did not come about partly because of near-death experiences much like the ones with which I have been dealing.

What have you found the attitude of physicians to be toward these experiences?

Again, as in the case of ministers, physicians are an enormously varied group of human beings, made up of individuals with different backgrounds, interests, and personalities. So, predictably, the response from them has been quite diverse. Nonetheless, it falls fairly neatly into about four categories, which makes the task of discussion somewhat easier.

The first group consists of physicians who have had this experience themselves. Their attitude toward these experiences does not seem to be any different from that of anyone else who has had a near-death experience. A point that two physicians have made in relating their own accounts is that, despite the overwhelming reality of what they were experiencing, there was little in their scientific background that had prepared them for understanding it, or that gave them a language in which to express it. When I asked one doctor about his attitude to his own out-of-body experience, he answered, "As a scientist, I would've thought it couldn't happen. But it really did!"

A second group consists of the doctors who have contacted me to tell me of their own patients who had reported these experiences. Several physicians have remarked that they, too, had been collecting these accounts, had been quite baffled by them, and were glad to find out that others had been doing research into this area.

Yet another group has expressed a religious attitude toward these phenomena. They feel that the occurence of near-death experiences confirms their own religious faith that there is a continuation of life after physical death.

A fourth group consists of physicians who feel that near-death experiences are reducible to medical phenomena with which we are already familiar. They feel, in short, that they can explain near-death experiences on the basis of what we already know scientifically about physiology and/or psychology.

What are some examples of known medical phenomena which have been proposed as explanations of these experiences?

There is an almost endless list of conditions known to medicine which can produce experiences that, in one respect or another, resemble the phenomena reported in some near-death encounters. In *Life After Life*, I discussed certain pharmacological, physiological, neurological, and psychological explanations of near-death experiences. It would be pointless to explore each of the possible explanations separately, but I will remark that the two fields of medicine which seem to be among the most fertile grounds from which phenomena similar to near-death experiences are derived are anesthesiology and neurology. I am aware, of course, that sensations like that of being drawn down a dark tunnel are often reported by persons being placed under anesthetics—especially ether. Yet, I do not believe that anesthetic effects constitute a valid, complete explanation of near-death experiences, since very few of my subjects were under any sort of anesthetic at the time the experience took place.

Likewise, many neurologists have pointed out to me over the past several years that near-death experiences bear a certain resemblance to seizure disorders, particularly to temporal lobe seizures. Some obvious points of resemblance are: (1) People who have temporal lobe seizures may report that a "noise" heralds the onset of the episode. (2) The temporal lobe has a role in memory, and persons who have approached death may talk of panoramic memory.

One could continue almost indefinitely drawing further parallels. For example, one might postulate that the impression of intense light reported by these persons is the result simply of events caused by interference with oxygen supply to the occipital lobes (the area of the brain which is the "seat" of vision). I would like to add to the list (besides those, such as autoscopy, mentioned in *Life After Life*) the experiences reported to the famous neurosurgeon Dr. Wilder Penfield by some of his patients. In a classic series of experiments, Dr. Penfield stimulated certain areas of the brains of his patients while they were undergoing brain surgery. When he did this, he found that very vivid memories—actually a sort of reliving of events—would flood into the patient's consciousness. Precise, complete details of events which had occurred years before could be recovered.

Yet, I personally remain unconvinced that these well-known neurological phenomena "explain" near-death experiences. Consider the explanation in terms of seizures, for example. Such attempted explanations are almost invariably based upon the premise that "cerebral anoxia" (loss of oxygen to the brain) is the specific cause of the seizure discharge. However, this neglects the point that all the phenomena alluded to—the noise, the panoramic memory, and the light—have been experienced in the course of near-death encounters in which this cut-off of blood flow to the brain never took place. Remember that I emphasized from the beginning that I have dealt with some near-death experiences in which no apparent clinical death took place, and that these contain many of the same features as those in which there was such a "death." A simple review of the cases I have presented should make this point obvious.

Some might want to go further and try to explain near-death experiences in which the light, the review, and other phenomena were experienced without any compromise of brain oxygen supply by saying that in these cases it was the "stress" of the close encounter with death which set off the alleged brain events. My only feeling about this is that here the concept of "stress" has been so stretched as to be almost without any explanatory force. ("What *kind* of stress?", one might ask.)

It is quite easy to go on formulating explanations of this type endlessly. However, it is also all too easy to accept some such explanation as obvious without giving proper attention to elements of near-death experiences which do not fit the suggested explanation. For example, physicians have reported to me that they just can't understand how their patients could have described the things they did about the resuscitation efforts unless they really were hovering just below the ceiling. Numerous persons have told me that while they were out of their bodies during apparent "death," they witnessed events at a distance—even outside the hospital—which were later confirmed by the reports of independent observers. I think we ought at least to leave our minds open to the possibility that such uncanny corroborations might some day be produced under controlled experimental circumstances.

Finally, I must observe that such explanations do not impress people who have had these experiences themselves. One young man who was revived after an apparent "death" reflects:

It's funny. It's something that there is no way that it

could possibly exist, and yet you know without a doubt that it does.

Now I know that a lot of people will not believe this. . . . People will come out and say that scientifically this cannot exist. . . . But, you know what? It won't change a thing. Because just as sure as I'm sitting here now, if I died again today, virtually the same thing would happen, except that I could observe it better. And they can tell me it's not, and they can swear that it's not, and they can show me scientific evidence that it's not . . . and all I can do is say, "Well, I know where I've been."

What is your own personal attitude toward this research? Has it affected your life in any way?

I find that even after I have asserted that I am not trying to prove that there is life after death and have made all of my usual qualifying-remarks, some people with whom I talk are still not satisfied. They want to know what I, Raymond Moody, *feel*. I believe this is a legitimate question, as long as it is understood that this is a psychological matter and not a matter of a logical conclusion that I am trying to force on anyone else. To those who are interested in this autobiographical detail, I address the following remarks: I have come to accept as a matter of religious faith that there is a life after death, and I believe that the phenomenon we have been examining is a manifestation of that life.

However, far from being obsessed with death, I want to live. The persons I have interviewed would agree. The focus of their attention, as a result of having been through this experience, is on living. For we are all in this life now. At the same time, I hope to be able to apply what I have learned in this study to my life. I want to go on developing, as far as I can, in the areas of loving others and acquiring knowledge and wisdom.

Also, I am particularly concerned that near-death experiences not be perverted by using them as an excuse to form a new cult. This phenomenon should not be identified with me or with anyone else who has studied it. The near-death experience is very prevalent, and different perspectives are needed to cope with all of its complexities.

Finally, I have recently come to realize that my long contact with this research has resulted in my having a rather unusual distinction: A large percentage of my friends have been dead! Through talking with so many people, I have begun to realize how near to death we all are in our daily lives. More than ever now I am very careful to let each person I love know how I feel.

EPILOGUE

In Book VII of *The Republic*, the philosopher Plato (428-348 B.C.) produced for us a very powerful and beautiful allegory, which has since come to be known as the myth of the Cave. It takes the form of a dialogue between Plato's old teacher, Socrates, and another man, Glaucon. I quote this remarkable parable here without further comment. Its relevance is obvious.

Picture men dwelling in a sort of subterranean cavern with a long entrance open to the light on its entire width. Conceive them as having their legs and necks fettered from childhood, so that they remain in the same spot, able to look forward only, and prevented by the fetters from turning their heads. Picture further the light from a fire burning higher up and at a distance behind them, and between the fire and the prisoners and above them a road along which a low wall has been built, as the exhibitors of puppet shows have partitions before the men themselves, above which they show the puppets.

All that I see, he said.

See also, then, men carrying past the wall implements of all kinds that rise above the wall, and human images and shapes of animals as well, wrought in stone and wood and every material, some of these bearers presumably speaking and others silent.

A strange image you speak of, he said, and strange prisoners.

Like to us, I said. For, to begin with, tell me do you think that these men would have seen anything of themselves or of one another except the shadows cast from the fire on the wall of the cave that fronted them?

How could they, he said, if they were compelled to hold their heads unmoved through life?

And again, would not the same be true of the objects carried past them?

Surely.

If then they were able to talk to one another, do you not think that they would suppose that in naming the things that they saw they were naming the passing objects?

Necessarily.

And if their prison had an echo from the wall opposite them, when one of the passers-by uttered a sound, do you think that they would suppose anything else than the passing shadow to be the speaker?

By Zeus, I do not, said he.

Then in every way such prisoners would deem reality to be nothing else than the shadows of the artificial objects.

Quite inevitably, he said.

Consider, then, what would be the manner of the release and healing from these bonds and this folly if in the course of nature something of this sort should happen to them. When one was freed from his fetters and compelled to stand up suddenly and turn his head around and walk and to lift up his eyes to the light, and in doing all this felt pain and, because of the dazzle and glitter of the light, was unable to discern the objects whose shadows he formerly saw, what do you suppose would be his answer if someone told him that what he had seen before was all a cheat and an illusion, but that now, being nearer to reality and turned toward more real things, he saw more truly? And if also one should point out to him each of the passing objects and constrain him by questions to say what it is, do you not think that he would be at a loss and that he would regard what he formerly saw as more real than the things now pointed out to him?

Far more real, he said.

And if he were compelled to look at the light itself, would not that pain his eyes, and would he not turn away and flee to those things which he is able to discern and regard them as in very deed more clear and exact than the objects pointed out?

It is so, he said.

And if, said I, someone should drag him thence by force up the ascent which is rough and steep, and not let him go before he had drawn him out into the light of the sun, do you not think that he would find it painful to be so haled along, and would chafe at it, and when he came out into the light, that his eyes would be filled with its beams so that he would not be able to see even one of the things that we call real?

Why, no, not immediately, he said.

Then there would be need of habituation, I take it, to enable him to see the things higher up. And at first he would most easily discern the shadows and, after that, the likenesses or reflections in water of men and other things, and later, the things themselves, and from these he would go on to contemplate the appearances in the heavens and heaven itself, more easily by night, looking at the light of the stars and the moon, than by day the sun and the sun's light.

Of course.

And so, finally, I suppose, he would be able to look upon the sun itself and see its true nature, not by reflections in water or phantasms of it in an alien setting, but in and by itself in its own place.

Necessarily, he said.

And at this point he would infer and conclude that this it is that provides the seasons and the courses of the year and presides over all things in the visible region, and is in some sort the cause of all these things that they had seen.

Obviously, he said, that would be the next step.

Well then, if he recalled to mind his first habitation and what passed for wisdom there, and his fellow bondsmen, do you not think that he would count himself happy in the change and pity them?

He would indeed.

And if there had been honors and commendations among them which they bestowed on one another and prizes for the man who is quickest to make out the shadows as they pass and best able to remember their customary precedences, sequences, and coexistences, and so most successful in guessing at what was to come, do you think he would be very keen about such rewards, and that he would envy and emulate those who were honored by these prisoners and lorded it among them, or that he would feel with Homer and greatly prefer while living on earth to be serf of another, a landless man, and endure anything rather than opine with them and live that life?

Yes, he said, I think that he would choose to endure anything rather than such a life.

And consider this also, said I. If such a one should go down again and take his old place would he not get his eyes full of darkness, thus suddenly coming out of the sunlight?

He would indeed.

Now if he should be required to contend with these perpetual prisoners in 'evaluating' these shadows while his vision was still dim and before his eyes were accustomed to the dark—and this time required for habituation would not be very short—would he not provoke laughter, and would it not be said of him that he had returned from his journey aloft with his eyes ruined and that it was not worth while even to attempt the ascent? And if it were possible to lay hands on and to kill the man who tried to release them and lead them up, would they not kill him?

They certainly would, he said.[1]

[1]Edith Hamilton and Huntington Cairns, eds., *The Collected Dialogues of Plato*, trans. Paul Shorey, Bollingen Series 71 (New York: Pantheon Books, 1961), pp. 747-749.

APPENDIX:
METHODOLOGICAL
CONSIDERATIONS

I have received many inquiries of a methodological nature from persons who are interested in future research in the area of near-death phenomena. In addition, I have given much thought to methodological questions because I myself have an interest in logic and scientific method. I have found that these questions fall generally into four areas: classification, interviewing techniques, scientific method, and proposals for future study in this area. I would like to present some of my own reflections on these matters for whatever benefit they might be to anyone who has an interest in carrying out near-death studies and also for readers who, being of a scientific or logical frame of mind, might have particular queries to make along these lines.

I. Classification

As I have said, not everyone who has a close call with death reports having any experience at all; many report that they remember nothing whatsoever about their encounters. Some people even have an apparent clinical death and come back with no recollection of having had any conscious experience at all during that time. On the other hand, as I also mentioned, people have reported having experiences of the kind I have described even when they were not, as far as they knew, anywhere near death or even ill. Further, experiences of the kind I have dealt with have taken place under a wide spectrum of conditions which vary quite a bit with respect to what may be called (vaguely) the "closeness" with which death was approached.

Such factors could generate a certain confusion in the terminology employed in discussing these reports. Hence, I would like to propose some definitions and a classification scheme which may be of some help in lessening the confusion.

First, one might define a "near-death experience" as any conscious perceptual experience which takes place during a near-death encounter. A "near-death encounter" might in turn be defined as an event in which a person could very easily die or be killed (and even may be so close as to be believed or pronounced clinically dead) but nonetheless survives, and continues physical life.

A classification of "near-death experiences" could, I suppose, be developed from such lists of common elements of near-death experiences as the one I have set out in my earlier book. "Near-death encounters" may be classified minimally into the following kinds of situations.

A. A person finds himself in a situation in which he

could very easily be killed or die, even though he subsequently escapes without injury. He reports having a subjective feeling of certainty that he would be dead very shortly. Yet, against all odds, he lives through the ordeal unharmed.

B. A person is gravely ill or injured, even to the point where his physicians give him no chance to live. Nonetheless, he never undergoes an apparent clinical death and, indeed, goes on eventually to recover.

C. A person is gravely ill or severely injured and, at some point, some of the criteria for clinical death are satisfied. For example, his heart may stop beating and/or he may stop breathing. His doctors may actually believe that he is dead. However, resuscitation procedures are immediately begun, and no one actually *pronounces* him dead. The resuscitation measures work and he lives.

D. A person is gravely ill or severely injured and, as in (C) above, at some point some of the criteria for clinical death are satisfied. Resuscitation measures are begun but do not seem to work, so they are abandoned. His doctors believe that he is dead and at some point he is actually pronounced dead. The death certificate may even be signed. However, at a later time, even *after* he has been declared dead, resuscitation measures are resumed for some reason and he is revived.

E. A person is gravely ill or severely injured and at some point some of the criteria for clinical death are satisfied. Resuscitation measures are not even begun because the case seems hopeless. His doctors believe that he is dead and at some point he is actually pronounced dead. The death certificate may even be signed. However, at a later time, even *after* he has been declared dead, resuscitation measures are begun and he is revived.

F. A person is gravely ill or severely injured and at some point some of the criteria for clinical death are satisfied. Resuscitation measures may or may not be begun, but if they are, they are abandoned, and he is believed or even pronounced dead. At a later time, however, he defies the doctors by "snapping out of it" spontaneously, without resuscitation measures being used.

I have collected examples of near-death experiences which occurred in connection with each of the types of near-death encounters listed above except for (F). That is, none of my subjects who reported an experience had it during a "death" from which he spontaneously revived. Nonetheless, spontaneous "arousals" of this nature apparently do sometimes occur. I have talked to one person who spontaneously "woke up" after having been believed dead, even though he doesn't remember having an experience in the interim.

Some might ask whether the absence of any "spontaneous recovery" cases in my collection doesn't imply that near-death experiences are merely artifacts of the technique of resuscitation—that is, something which is somehow caused by the effect on the brain or body of the procedures employed. This seems unlikely to me, for the simple reason that near-death experiences have occurred in near-death encounters of types (A) and (B) in which resuscitation measures are *not* employed.

The descriptions of types (D) and (E) raise the question of why resuscitation measures would be begun or resumed after a person has already been declared dead. The reasons have varied in the cases I have collected which fall into these categories. For example, in one case, the patient's finger was seen to twitch several minutes after he had been declared dead. Resuscitation was begun and he lived. In another, the physician involved had given up and told the nurse, "Write out the death certificate for three fifteen and I'll sign it." Shortly thereafter he decided that he just couldn't face the young son and wife of the patient involved, since he knew the family personally. He felt he just had to try again. He did, and after another extended period of resuscitation attempts the patient "came back." In yet another case, one of the medical personnel present desperately tried to talk the physician into trying again. He did, and this time the attempt worked.

With regard to types (A) through (E), I can make the following remark. In general, it seems to me that there is a progression of what one might call the depth or "completeness" of the associated near-death experiences as one goes from type (A) through type (E) near-death encounters. For example, a person who has an experience during a type (A) encounter seems typically only to report seeing his life flash before him, or only to feel that he was out of his body briefly, while those who are involved in progressively closer calls seem typically to report more of the elements which have been described. The most vivid and complete experiences I have heard took place in connection with type (D) and (E) encounters. On the other hand:

(1) This is certainly not a *necessary* correlation as far as I can tell, even in my own collection of cases. For I have met with persons who were actually believed dead and resuscitated but remember few or no elements of the experience, as well as with persons who had more complete experiences even during type (A) or (B) encounters.

(2) Establishing general correlations between type of encounter and "depth" of experience could only be done exactly through scientific studies of a type which I have not carried out, but which I will attempt to characterize later in this Appendix.

II. Interviewing Techniques

It could be said (and truly) that the procedure of conducting interviews is a notoriously unreliable way of gathering scientific information. Thus, not surprisingly, I am often asked by interested medical professionals, "How do you go about interviewing these people?"

Now, it occurs to me in retrospect that this question is ambiguous; it has at least two distinct meanings, and I want to discuss both. The first meaning is this: "Isn't it possible that, by asking the right questions, you could plant these stories in people's minds?"

Thus formulated, this question raises a very real and interesting point. Questions *do* often suggest answers. I think it may be helpful in addressing this more precisely to make a few remarks about the concept of a question generally. In effect, questions are complex functions of language. It is probably impossible to find a question in which there is no statemental (i.e., "information-conveying") component at all, either explicitly within the verbal formulation itself or implicitly in the context in which the question is asked.

So I would say this. From a certain point of view, the technique of the interview is flawed scientifically: since it involves asking questions and questions convey information, the issue might theoretically always arise whether the information which appears to be derived from the interviewee might not originate with the interviewer through his questions or other actions.

Since I have a great interest in logic and methodology generally, my first impulse for a long time was to answer the original ambiguous question as though it had this first meaning I have just discussed. Sometimes, though, my answer seemed to leave the medical student or doctor who asked the question somehow unsatisfied. Thinking back on it realizing as I do that many persons in the medical field themselves have a high level of anxiety about the subject of death, it occurs to me that some were probably asking a very different question indeed, namely: "How in the world do you broach such an *obscene* topic as his own clinical death with a person?"

So the original question can be resolved into at least two distinct questions, the first having a more purely logical and the second a more purely emotional impact. My interviewing techniques have been developed in response to both of these aspects.

Let me say that when I started my research it was something which apparently only a very few other persons had ever done. Consequently, no manual had been written on how to interview persons who had come back from the dead. I had to learn by experience (and, indeed, I am still learning), but I have formulated some very general rules and guidelines. I fully expect and hope that they will be modified and added to by other researchers.

The first "rule" is just this: Be sympathetic. People are reticent to talk about these things for fear of being ridiculed or disbelieved by others. I'm sure that I would never have gotten anywhere had I used a hostile, inquisitorial kind of approach with people by trying to point out contradictions in what they say, etc.

Secondly, if you feel uncomfortable talking with people about their experiences, remember that this may well be your own fear of death coming through. I have found that persons who have been through near-death experiences seldom have the awful kind of dread of death which many of us seem to have.

Thirdly, in light of the difficulty about questions mentioned above, I think that the very best one can do is to formulate questions which emphasize the imperative function as much as is possible. One should begin the interview with open-ended questions and save the more specific questions for a later point.

I always start with as neutral a question as possible, for instance, "Could you tell me what happened to you?" In a couple of cases I did ask very loaded questions. This was because the persons being interviewed were still in hospital beds recovering from the illnesses which had led to their "deaths." They were in a great deal of pain and yet obviously wanted very much to talk. I led them on a bit, I confess, because I wanted in a way to get the interviews over with as quickly as possible so that they would be more comfortable In these cases, I asked them about whether certain elements of the composite near-death experience had been present in their experiences. However, if they did not recall them, they said so. This, in a way, gives me encouragement.

III. Scientific Method

One difficulty in considering accounts of near-death experiences as evidence for an afterlife is that they are anecdotal reports. The scientific method greatly restricts the use of human testimony as evidence. There are at least three good reasons for this.

(1) People sometimes lie.
(2) People sometimes misremember or misinterpret what happens to them.
(3) People sometimes have hallucinations or delusions, especially when under stress.

Indeed, given the general fallibility of human reporting, some might even say that such reports as I have collected are utterly without merit.

However, some counterbalancing remarks need to be made here. First of all, it has happened time and time again that science has slipped up in not listening more carefully to human testimony. For example, until the early decades of the nineteenth century the possibility of meteorites (rocks that fall to the earth from outer space) was widely dismissed and debunked by science. Still the folk legends of stones falling from heaven persisted, despite the insistence of scientists that this was impossible. (They argued that stones could not fall from the heavens since there were no stones in the heavens to fall.) Finally, two Princeton professors witnessed a meteorite fall and took the pieces they gathered back to their college to study.

In general, then, the dismissal of human testimony as evidence is a two-edged sword. Let's suppose that it is true that, since people often lie, misinterpret, etc., we may avoid error by disallowing human testimony as evidence. However, it must then be just as true that, since people often speak honestly and interpret correctly, we may miss the truth by refusing to heed what they say.

Furthermore, it sometimes happens that human testimony is all we have to go on at a certain time with respect to certain issues. Survival after bodily death is certainly one of these. Of course, the reports of persons who have come close to death do not constitute proof or even evidence of that issue. Still, given our curiosity, it may be that the best we can do is to ask people who have been close to death to tell us about it. If, as we have found to be the case, their independent reports agree quite well, we have a right to be impressed by that fact, even though it does not constitute proof.

Finally, the fact that a widespread phenomenon is not handled very well by our current scientific methodologies and conceptual systems should not lead us simply to dismiss it. Ideally, this fact should provoke us to try to come up with new concepts and new techniques of discovery—ones which do not contradict, but rather build upon and go beyond those to which we are accustomed.

As I have been the first to admit, the study which I have done is not strictly a "scientific" one, for many reasons. For one, the sample of subjects I have studied is not truly random, but has been selected by many factors other than chance. Also as we saw, my study consists of anecdotal reports, which are not admissible evidence scientifically.

Some of these factors are remediable; they stem from limitations on my own resources and time. However, there are other problems arising from the very nature of the subject matter under investigation here which would make it exceedingly difficult, if not impossible, to carry out an unquestionably scientific study under adequately controlled experimental conditions. These problems are both moral and procedural. Obviously, we can't put statistically significant numbers of people into a state of clinical death in order to be able to record their impressions upon a hoped-for resuscitation!

The actual clinical situations involved are not controlled experimental environments, but rather medical emergencies. The first duty of a physician and the other medical personnel in such circumstances is, and ought only to be, to give therapy to the patient, to try to revive him. It is not their duty to perform experiments related to the nature or validity of near death experiences.

It seems that the only thing that would be clearly within the limits of moral acceptability would be to collect data, in effect, after the fact. Data quite often come into existence in the course of resuscitation attempts, not because a conscious attempt has been made to collect them for scientific purposes, but rather as the more or less secondary result of the therapeutic and/or diagnostic measures taken. For example, clinical records often may show why a person "died" or came close to death, how long he was in this state, how he was brought back from it, what his first responses were upon being brought back, what drugs were administered to him, etc. Also, "harder" data might exist in the form of any tracings from EEG or EKG machines used, recorded temperature and blood pressure readings, results of any laboratory tests which were done before or after the emergency, and so on. It is conceivable that advances in resuscitation technology or instrumentation might make such data even more reliable and easier to come by in the near future.

IV. Preliminary Suggestions for Future Research

Granted the availability of data of the type mentioned above, and possibly of other kinds, how can near-death experiences be studied? One possibility is the formation of an inter-disciplinary study group in which interested representatives from many fields will work together. Among the fields which can be represented are medicine, physiology, pharmacology, philosophy, psychology, psychiatry, anthropology, comparative religion, theology, and the ministry.

A group of this nature could address itself to a large number of tasks. Among them are the following:

A. Examples of near-death experiences could be collected in a more systematic and organized way. For example, doctors and hospital staff members could be contacted and requested to ask patients whom they resuscitate whether they had experiences and to report the response. Or, the request could be to permit a team of investigators to approach the patient and ascertain whether he had an experience. Note: The cases in which no experience at all was reported would be important, too, for the sake of comparative studies.

B. Clinical records of the "after the fact" type described above could be searched out and compiled for as many of the near-death experiences as possible. This could be valuable as corroboration that the person who describes an experience did "die" or come near death. In addition, this data might make it possible to compile a more reliable statistical cross section of the medical status of persons having experiences and help to reveal whether there is a pattern to be found with respect to cause of death, age at time of the experience, methods of resuscitation employed, and so forth. A statistically better correlation than I have been able to make might be established between the length of time a subject is in a physiological crisis and the depth of his experience.

C. A search might be made for instances in which independent corroboration of a very persuasive type exists. "Ideal" cases of this type might be constructed, for example, along lines similar to these.

(1) In an emergency room, an individual, Mr. A, is being treated for a severe medical crisis by doctors and medical personnel. Since his treatment has continued for some time, there has been adequate time for instrumentation to be carefully and correctly set up, so that the medical team can monitor his status. Accordingly, gauges are giving information about his blood pressure and respiration while an EKG monitors his heart function and an EEG is keeping the personnel informed of the activity of his brain. Precisely at a certain time, which is carefully recorded by those on hand, Mr. A undergoes a cardiac

and respiratory arrest and this is both clinically apparent
and recorded on the instrumentation. Someone there
both witnesses and records that Mr. A's pupils dilate and
that his body temperature begins to fall. Resuscitation
attempts are begun immediately and, after a precisely
timed interval, succeed. Mr. A recovers.

Soon thereafter, Mr. A tells his physicians that he had a
fantastic experience while he was "dead"; that he seemed
to get out of his body and to witness the resuscitation
attempts from another point of view. He reports that
while in this state he left the room entirely and went to
another place where he witnessed an unusual event taking place, which he proceeds to describe in detail.

Not only do the medical personnel agree that Mr. A's
account of their actions in resuscitating him is accurate,
but an immediate check establishes that the event which
he says he witnessed while outside of the room *did* take
place almost exactly where and as he said it did. Further,
it can be established that the event took place at the
precise time when Mr. A is known to have been in a state
of clinical death, as supported by flat EEG and EKG
tracings.

(2) Suppose two or more persons undergo a clinical
"death" simultaneously and are resuscitated. This could
happen, for example, in the course of a mass accident of
some kind, or if two or more persons just happened to
"die" in the same hospital at the same time. Suppose
further that they were to both report as soon as they came
back—while still isolated from one another while in the
out-of-body state. The content of this alleged communication could be collected from both independently while
they were still isolated from each other. If this checked
out, it would certainly be significant and interesting.

Neither of the two types of cases described above,
however, would necessarily constitute proof of life after
death. Extrasensory perception could be a possible explanation of any cases of these two "ideal" types. Someone
could always raise the possibility that the subjects were

able to observe what they did, not by actually leaving their bodies, but by telepathically picking up the thoughts of observers who were physically at the scene.

I am not suggesting that it is likely that researchers will come up with cases which are as perfect as the ones outlined above. I do suggest that investigators formulate a series of theoretical models. Using them as a standard, the investigators could compare actual cases to the modes and to one another and devise a "yardstick" for classifying actual encounters.

D. Investigators trained in psychology might carry out in-depth interviews with subjects who came near death. Valuable clues might be revealed as to how the patient's experience changed him, to what degree his interpretation of it was shaped by his emotional makeup and background, and so on. Comparisons of the results could reveal how persons reporting near-death experiences differ among themselves and if they differ from the population as a whole.

E. Separate elements of near-death experiences may well have to be studied and/or explained separately. For example, suppose that the "buzzing" noise people report at the moments near death turned out to have a particular physiological explanation. It would not follow that any other elements in the experience—say, the encounter with relatives and friends who had died before—would have the same type of explanation.

F. An extensive search could be made for cases of near-death experiences from contexts outside that of modern Western society. The aid of anthropologists might be enlisted in collecting near-death experiences from the members of very different cultures. A careful review of historical literature might turn up instances from our own Western tradition. An expert in the field of comparative religion might be able to point out parallels in the many religions of the world. The possibilities are endless.

G. Persons who have had near-death experiences could be brought together in groups to discuss their experiences among themselves. I have done this many times now and find it has many advantages. Until now most people who have had this experience have thought they were all alone or that their cases were so rare they would never find someone else who had had a similar experience.

This impression is certainly dispelled intellectually and emotionally in a group. Also, the effability gap is partly bridged. People say that for the first time they feel they have met someone who really understands and empathizes, despite the limitations of language. At the close of a group experience of this type, one man enthused, "That was the most fantastic evening of my life. I was discussing things I usually can't even talk about." I have found that as an observer in these groups I have been able to understand in a better way than before what a near-death experience may be like.

I would like to give two pointers here. A group of three persons who have had this experience is about the optimum size, it seems to me. Also, it can be helpful to have the spouses of the participants present. They have often themselves had trouble understanding this experience of their wife or husband, and having another person tell about a similar experience might help.

H. Finally, I feel that close attention should be paid to the arguments of those who see this phenomenon as explicable in terms of natural causes and scientific concepts with which we are already familiar—for example, residual electrical activity of the brain. For, it goes without saying that natural science has brought us a long way in our understanding of the universe.

At the same time, I think that one should avoid the temptation to accept simple-minded natural explanations without putting them to any sort of test. I have heard many people make remarks to the effect that it is just "obvious" that the explanation of near-death phenomena is, for example, cerebral anoxia (that is, loss of oxygen supply to the brain). It is quite easy to come up with any number of possible natural explanations of this type off the top of one's head. What is lacking, I would suggest, is any particular experimental demonstration that any given explanation of this type is correct. As I pointed out in *Life After Life*, what makes me doubt simplistic explanations of this type is that I can find certain near-death experiences in which each explanation which has ever been proposed to me just doesn't fit the facts or situation surrounding those particular experiences.

After all, there is a difference between "explaining" something and merely "explaining it away." The latter involves reducing an apparently new phenomenon to an old one, or saying that the new is really just a special case of phenomena with which we are already familiar (or think we are). It seems to me that we should always be at least open to the possibility that what seem to be new phenomena are true anomalies—items or facts which just do not fit into the structure of previously articulated world views. For it is certainly just this openness to the occurrence of anomalies in our experience which has historically been one of the greatest incentives to the advancement of human understanding.

V. Some Concluding Remarks

Let me close this section on methodology with a few random remarks which might be of value to any future researchers of this phenomenon. First, I think that researchers should avoid the tendency to dismiss near-death experiences as unworthy topics for research just because certain elements in them conflict with dearly held assumptions about the nature of the world.

I admit that near-death experiences contain aspects which, from our present perspective, are completely incomprehensible. For example, apparent inconsistencies arise regarding time. The contemporary Western view of time is that it is an intimate feature of the physical universe, that it flows forever in a linear fashion. Yet people who come back from near-death experiences assert that "time stood still."

I don't have any answers for people who ask questions about these apparent anomalies. Nonetheless, as I am sure quite a few physicists and philosophers would agree, the common sense concept of time generates many paradoxes just in itself, regardless of the occurrence of near-death visions. The additional dilemmas posed by a consideration of near-death experiences are just a drop in the bucket.

I also caution researchers to avoid the tendency to assume that just because someone has been "dead," and has had an experience, he must know everything about what happens on the other side. No one has come back feeling that he was infallible or omniscient with regard to the afterlife because of his experience. Most have expressed genuine bafflement about many of the things they went through. In other words, if someone is fallible here, before he has his experience, there is no reason to assume that he is going to be infallible after he returns from "death."

Finally, it would more likely advance our understanding of the human mind if persons who are interested in doing research on near-death experiences would tackle only one aspect at a time. I feel that a huge research project geared to the aim of proving that there is life after death through study of near-death experiences would likely be ill-conceived and, at the current level of our understanding, overly ambitious. My own feeling is that, *within the context of science alone*, there may never be a proof of life after death.

On the other hand, I believe that a large number of individual research projects, each one set up with the aim of testing some particular, more limited experimental hypothesis, would be likely to yield scientifically usable data about near-death experiences. Further, I believe that possibly the end result of the accumulation of particular bits of knowledge through these individual, painstaking attempts would be a fading away of the issue of whether there is life after death, without a single, dramatic scientific proof ever being given.

Let me illustrate what I mean by an anology. Though most of us believe in the existence of atoms, there never was—to my knowledge—a single, dramatic proof of this. Rather, what happened seems to have been a long, historical development of thought relating to these hypothetical entities. Even hundreds of years before Christ, Greek philosophers such as Democritus had conceived of an atomic theory of matter. They postulated the existence of minute, "indivisible" particles of matter. They did this partly on the basis of abstract, deductive, and metaphysical reasoning, but partly also on the basis of their own empirical observations of various natural phenomena such as diffusion and the imperceptably gradual wearing away of large objects. Through centuries of development, during which the concept of the atom was altered and techniques for the verification of its existence were correspondingly modified, the atomic theory has slowly come to be widely accepted.

I believe it lies within the realm of possibility that in a similar fashion, almost everyone may eventually come to accept intellectually, even without definite proof, that there is another dimension of existence into which the soul passes at death. Remember that it is our own anxiety about whether death is final which shows through when we challenge a person who has had such an experience to *prove* that there is life after death. Most people who have had near-death experiences don't seem interested in proving it to other people. One woman psychiatrist who had a near-death experience told me, "People who have had these experiences *know*. People who haven't should *wait*."

BIBLIOGRAPHY

Near-Death Experiences and Parallels

Barrett, William. *Death-Bed Visions*. London: Methuen & Co., 1926.

Bede. *A History of the English Church and People*, trans. Leo Sherley-Price. Harmondsworth, England: Penguin Books, 1968.

Canning, Raymond R. "Mormon Return-From-The-Dead Stories." *Utah Academy Proceedings*, XLII (1965). Cited in *The Sociology of Death*, by Glenn M. Vernon. N.Y.: The Ronald Press Co., 1470, pp. 64-65.

Delacour, Jean-Baptiste. *Glimpses of the Beyond*. N.Y.: Delacorte Press, 1973.

DeQuincey, Thomas. *Confessions of An English Opium Eater With Its Sequels Suspiria De Profundis and The English Mail Coach*, ed. Malcolm Elwin. London: Macdonald & Co., 1956.

Dobson, M., et. al. "Attitudes and Long Term Adjustment of Patients Surviving Cardiac Arrest." *British Medical Journal*, Vol. 3 (1971), pp. 207-212.

Hamilton, Edith, and Huntington Cairns, eds. *The Collected Dialogues of Plato*. Bolingen Series LXXI. New York: Pantheon Books, 1963.

Hunter, R. C. A. "On The Experience Of Nearly Dying." *American Journal of Psychiatry*, 124 (1967), pp. 122-126.

Jackson, Kenneth H. *A Celtic Miscellany*. Harmondsworth, England: Penguin Books, 1971.

James, William. *The Varieties of Religious Experience*. New York: New American Library, 1958.

Jung, C. G. *Memories, Dreams, Reflections*, ed. Aniela Jaffé and trans. Richard and Clara Winston. New York: Vintage Books, 1965.

Kübler-Ross, Elisabeth. *On Death and Dying*. New York: Macmillan Publishing Co., Inc., 1969.

Neihardt, John G. *Black Elk Speaks*. New York: Pocket Books, 1972.

Noyes, Russell. "The Experience of Dying." *Psychiatry*, Vol. 35 (1972), pp. 174-184.

Noyes, Russell and Roy Kletti. "Depersonalization In The Face Of Life-Threatening Danger: A Description." *Psychiatry*, Vol. 39 (1976), pp. 19-27.

Osis, Karl. *Deathbed Observations by Physicians and Nurses*. Parapsychological Monographs, No. 3. N.Y.: Parapsychology Foundation, 1961.

Osis, Karl. "What Do The Dying See." *Newsletter of the American Society For Psychical Research*, 24 (Winter 1975).

Pandey, Caro. "The Need For The Psychological Study of Clinical Death." *Omega*, Vol. 2 (1971), pp. 1-9.

Ritchie, George. *Return From Tomorrow*. Lincoln, Virginia: Chosen Books, 1977.

Tylor, Edward B. *Primitive Culture*, Vol. II. New York: Henry Holt and Company, 1874.

Uekshuell, K. "Unbelievable For Many, But Actually A True Occurrence." *Moscow Journal* (late 19th Century). Translated and reprinted in *Orthodox Life*, Vol. 26, No. 4 (1976), pp. 1-36.